Into

Dedication

This book is dedicated to those who have heard the call to enter God's New Day and have left their comfort zone in life and ministry. They have inspired us with their humility, courage and willingness to pay the price for God's Kingdom.

Also, it is dedicated to those who God is raising up to become the generation that will reap the harvest as they take the Good News to the ends of the earth.

Into the Land

Mike Dwight

New Wine Press

Published by New Wine Press

An imprint of RoperPenberthy Publishing Ltd,
19 Egerton Place, Weybridge,
Surrey KT13 0PF

ISBN 978 1 910848 13 5

Cover design by Paul Stanier

Typeset by Avocet Typeset, Somerton, Somerset TA11 6RT

Printed in the United Kingdom

Contents

Acknowledgements

I must begin by thanking those, particularly in WEC International, who have encouraged me to seek first God's Kingdom and whose lives have shown me what this meant. Encouragement may appear so ordinary but is in fact a precious jewel within the body of Christ.

I want to thank Andrew Bowker for his insight, wisdom and commitment steering me through the writing of this book. My appreciation must also go to Nathan Dudgeon for his keen editorial comments which have challenged me to think through many key issues and to Maureen Trowbridge for proofreading this book.

Finally, I want to thank J. Stuart Reid for writing the foreword. His heart for the church and worldwide mission has never diminished and his passion to preach and teach and follow Jesus has been a blessing to countless people in the UK and abroad.

Foreword

The Scots have a saying, "Guid gear gangs intae wae bouk" which being translated means, "Good stuff is often packed into small things." This is surely true of this book. Its length will not tire you but its content will certainly impact you.

The church in the west finds itself by and large in a hard desert-like place and its strange desire to want to be approved by the world could lead to panic and to doing anything that 'works', ie, grows it numerically to get out of its impotence!

Mike Dwight after decades of planting churches, lecturing and pastoring in the UK and the Far East has given us the steps for the way ahead, which are not painless but they are proven. Using the story of Moses and his encounter with God in the desert, he shows us the only place where hope and help can be found.

This is an essential reminder that this generation needs to find its bearings. This is a strong prophetic word to our culture of fads, hype and fudge. Mike points to our only hope – a fresh experience of God Himself and His grace to work in us and for us. God and His gospel cannot fail, therefore we must raise our heads and re-focus on Him. This book was not born out of theoretical or academic musings but out of years of missionary work, full of trials, disappointments and dogged perseverance.

I have known Mike Dwight for over 40 years, he has always been seeking treasure and here he has hit bed rock and struck gold! These old truths are perennially new. It seems pretty obvious but Mike says it – God Himself must revive His people but we must press out from the desert to possess the land the Lord has for each of us. It is not a call to, "Let go and let God", but to actively press on to spiritual maturity and a fresh anointing of the Spirit that God desires to give.

This call is not an impossible dream as is made clear from many vivid illustrations from men and women from church history and from the contemporary lives of drug users who have been set free by Christ. The great fact is that God can do it in our lives today, His mercies are new every morning.

This is a very challenging yet joyful, hope-filled book, as God calls us to total commitment to His ways. From this book you get the overwhelming certainty that Mike has been mastered by the sheer god-ness of God and this shouts and sings throughout the book. Please don't read it quickly. Read it listening not just for the heart and wisdom of the author but for the voice of the Spirit.

The truth of this book is timeless. To the wise, true godliness never went out of fashion! This is an urgently needed message to the whole church and it is as needful for the last week of our Christian life on earth as it is for our first. We are greatly indebted to Mike Dwight for the truth written here. We desperately need books like this to get us back on track today and to see again 'where true gold can be found' not just for us but for an impoverished lost world around us. Its truths need to be shouted from the mountain tops.

J. Stuart Reid, Bible teacher and former church leader

Introduction

In my early missionary days, the story of Don and Carol Richardson's ministry to the Sawi tribe living in Papua New Guinea made a deep impression on me. In 1962 the Sawi lived as Stone Age cannibals. The Richardsons learnt the language, observed their culture and gradually began to share the Gospel with them. When Don shared the Easter story and described Judas Iscariot, there was a hushed silence. For three years he kept close company with Jesus, shared the same food, travelled the same road and became part of the inner group of disciples – only to betray Jesus with a kiss.

Suddenly there was a roar of approval from the Sawi tribe. As a cannibal tribe one of their prized tactics was to 'fatten with friendship for an unsuspected kill'. Judas was a hero, a super Sawi, and Jesus the object of his treachery meant nothing to them. The Richardsons' longing for the Sawi tribe to receive new life seemed further away than ever.

A few months later, three tribes in that area fought ferociously. Blood, death and the monotonous drum of war became routine. When the dreadful hostility had run its course the Richardsons learnt how, according to ancestral beliefs, peace was obtained. Embedded in their culture was the means of peace, offering a child. They offered a child.

Each cannibal tribe brought a child as a peace offering.

But instead of being sacrificed, each tribe would care for the other's child, so maintaining the peace. The child was called a 'tarop child'.

Isaiah 9:6 'For to us a child is born, to us a son is given..... Prince of Peace'.

Don retold the Easter story explaining that Judas had betrayed God's 'peace child'. From being a hero he was now the worst villain. The Sawi tribe were strangers to our Judaeo-Christian heritage but God had providentially ordained what Richardson termed redemptive analogies within the Sawi culture. It was a new day for the Sawi tribe. Individuals began to understand and believe in Jesus, God's 'tarop' child. Within a short while, the tribe built a thousand seat hut for meetings called 'The House of Peace'.

The new day for the Sawi tribe has been one of many testimonies that have gripped my heart. God breaking through the darkness and shining His light of life and truth into an otherwise hopeless situation; surely this is for us today!

God has been challenging me to focus on Moses and Israel's preparation to leave the desert and enter into the land of Canaan. This book will be looking at some of the challenges and lessons of this journey, both to encourage and sharpen us as we believe and prepare for the coming of God's new day.

My prayer is that *Into the Land* will touch your heart as it has touched mine in writing it. From the depths of despair Don and Carol Richardson saw into the heart of God who loves to surprise us and make all things new.

John 5:17 Jesus said to them 'My Father is always at work to this very day, and I, too, am working'

On hearing Don share the Gospel, an old man from the Sawi tribe recalled some ancestral words:

'When immortality returns to mankind, those who learn its secrets first will come over the mountains and tell you that secret. Their skins will be white because they are continually renewed like the skin of a snake. Be sure to listen to them when they come, otherwise, my skin your skin, immortality will pass you by.'

Even when the Sawi tribe were totally unaware of it, God was at work to bring in His new day among them. He is our unchanging God who is the same yesterday, today and forever.

CHAPTER 1

Time to look up

There is a growing sense among many that God is about to pour out His Spirit afresh into various desperate situations around the world, including a dark and spiritually barren Europe. For some this glorious hope may induce comments like 'just open your eyes and look around today's world, does it really look like this is about to happen?' For others less critical it may be downgraded to mere wishful thinking.

If we're honest, there are occasions when we visit both lines of thought. In those moments the tabloids and current news grip our hearts with fear, and fear inevitably leads us to take our eyes off Jesus. In the United Kingdom there is a steady stream of negative comments about Christianity. They often highlight declining congregations, and an outdated and detached leadership locked into the past. This can all too easily give us the impression that God and His leadership have no relevance, influence and power in today's world

Recently, I re-watched C.S. Lewis's 'The Lion, the Witch and the Wardrobe'. The Pevensie children, Peter, Susan, Edmund and Lucy had no idea of the magical journey ahead of them. In the darkness of the old country house where they are sent, the children stumble through an old wardrobe into the land of Narnia. A White Witch held Narnia under an enchantment which made it always winter and never Christmas.

Despite this, there were those in Narnia who believed winter would turn into spring and summer and the wonder of Christmas enjoyed the whole year. However, no one understood the timing of this or the need for Aslan to lay down his life sacrificially. His death and subsequent resurrection defeated the White Witch. For us this reflects so beautifully the supreme victory of Jesus through his perfect sacrifice and resurrection through the power of the Holy Spirit opening the door for God's new day.

My heart rejoiced as I realised afresh that although there are times when all may appear dark, despondent and hopeless, winter can turn to spring, summer and harvest. God's shaft of light piercing the darkness was supremely seen as it shone upon those shepherds in Luke 2:10-12. Heaven opened and the angels, bringing God's message, spoke clearly amidst the glory of God:

'Do not be afraid, I bring you good news of great joy that will be for all people. Today in the town of David a Saviour has been born to you, who is Christ the Lord'.

For about 400 years prior to events in Luke chapter two, there was very little evidence of God's presence. However, something was about to change, reflecting the encouraging words in Psalm 24 **'lift up your heads'**. In today's very challenging and disturbing world, could there be a repeat of God's glory and news of salvation breaking through into the hearts of men and women? Could it be that God is preparing us for His Spirit to break out, turning winter into spring, summer and harvest? Surely now is the time to reflect upon the Psalmist's encouragement.

Is there a stirring of the Spirit of God in our hearts? Is the Spirit of God causing us to reflect on the truth that over the centuries, from that moment in Luke 2 onward, God has opened the heavens on so many occasions? These countless visitations have all borne witness to the truth of Isaiah 60:2, 3

'See darkness covers the earth and thick darkness is over the peoples, **but the Lord rises upon you and his glory appears over you.** *Nations will come to your light, and kings to the brightness of your dawn'.*

As you read the background to revivals over the centuries, you become very aware of how desperately dark and evil the days prior to revival were. They were times of great moral and spiritual darkness, political unrest and huge social need. Spiritual indifference and scepticism abounded. Religion was emptied of spiritual power. The masses were untouched by the church, and in high society the mention of religion was ridiculed. Lives were grossly immoral, drunken and foul. Marriage was sneered at. Church services declined, and buildings fell into disrepair. Lawless mobs ransacked and pillaged, burning houses, flinging open prisons, and the criminal element grew large and unrestrained:

When the Holy Spirit breathes life into verses like Isaiah 60:2 and 3 something changes and darkness, real and terrifying as it is, is now replaced by a fresh vision of God. This vision widens beyond our immediate locality to the world at large and God's parish.

When revival broke out in Wales in 1904 it was for more than Wales. The wind of the Spirit carried the revival fire to many nations as the wonderful news reached prayer groups in many parts of the world. Hunger and thirst for

God deepened. The flame of the Spirit burned in ever increasing circles of influence: in England and Scotland, Scandinavia and Europe, South Africa, India, Korea, China, Indonesia, Japan, South America, Australia and New Zealand.

A personal perspective

Over six years ago my wife and I were concluding our ministry of overseeing church planting teams across South-East Asia. That ministry, like most, had its ups and downs. There was the privilege of seeing churches planted in totally new places where the Gospel had never previously been preached. There were also the struggles, conflicts and failures that brought us to our knees with a fresh desire to meet with Jesus and experience renewal and yes revival in our hearts. But moments of darkness and despair occur not just from looking around at today's world, but also from looking within and seeing the worldliness of our character and barrenness of our ministry. Because of this we acknowledged the need for God's light to shine into our darkness yet again. God began to do that in my heart. The years of ministry may have been fruitful in so many ways, but that is not the point, this is about tomorrow not yesterday. It is time now to re-focus; yes, being changed into Jesus' likeness and allowing Him to prepare our hearts for what is to come!

The still, small voice of the Spirit reminded me that, from a heavenly perspective, nothing has changed. God's nature, plan and purpose are consistent and unchanging. He is our faithful and compassionate God in every situation no matter how difficult. Whether to the Hebrew Christians struggling under persecution and an evil world or for us today, the Spirit of God is watering the truth of God's Word.

Hebrews 13:8, *'Jesus is the same yesterday, today and forever'*

John 17:24, *'Father, I want those you have given me to be with me where I am, and to see my glory, the glory you have given me because you loved me before the creation of the world.'*

CHAPTER 2

Learn from the desert but don't live there; move on

In the same way that the desert preceded Moses and Israel entering into the Promised Land, so it is for us today. Part of us wishes that we could bypass the desert and go straight into the land and God's new day. Yet we know that, as with Israel, God has so much to teach us before that moment becomes reality.

When I speak about God's new day, it does not mean that the daily work of the church is considered to be secondary. It also does not mean that revival is the only means of effectively spreading the Gospel. To me it means that there are seasons when the Holy Spirit is poured out in exceptional measure. Jesus demonstrated that in John 4. This chapter is not so much about the woman at the well as it is about the town of Sychar meeting Jesus and declaring:

> 'We no longer believe just because of what you said; now we have heard for ourselves, and we know that this man (Jesus) really is the Saviour of the world' (John 4:42).

The disciples were amazed and maybe confused. After all, this is Samaria. The Samaritans were despised by the

Jews! But central to this remarkable portion of Scripture are the words of Jesus:

John 4:35, *'Do you not say four months more and then the harvest? I tell you, open your eyes and look at the fields! They are ripe for harvest'.*

God can turn winter into harvest with one breath of His Spirit.

These times when winter is turned into harvest are exceptional times of unusual blessing and activity in the life of the church. I need to remind myself that these moments do not begin with renewed vision or evangelistic zeal, nor are they the product of a leaders' meeting or conference, but are something that God by His Spirit is doing *to* the church. The church in a particular location is ignited by the Spirit and sprung from this is a wider movement or awakening. It stimulates a deep concern about sin and their relationship with God among church members, backsliding Christians and unbelievers. This season is ordained by God. The Holy Spirit awakens the church to evangelise the lost, and causes the lost to see their desperate need of Jesus Christ as their Saviour and Lord.

Jonathan Edwards once reflected that revival is a sudden and unexpected outpouring of the Holy Spirit in which more are converted in one week than in one decade. Who wouldn't hunger and thirst for this to be repeated today?

Dr. Martyn Lloyd-Jones, considered by some as the greatest preacher in the United Kingdom since Charles Haddon Spurgeon, said in 1945, 'I long for revival comparable to that of the 18th Century. More and more I am convinced that there, and there alone, lies our hope'.

He saw the need for God to pour out His Spirit like He did at Pentecost. He not only prayed for this himself but encouraged his congregation to do the same.

It is this new day that has caught my heart:

- a day of heaven being opened and darkness being pushed back
- a day of seeing the glory of God and hearing the voice of God speak clearly and powerfully
- a day when hardened, cynical, despising hearts are wonderfully changed, as young and old, rich and poor, become aware that today, God's mercy and grace can still be received, and His day of salvation has not passed them by
- a day when we in the church not only believe in Jesus as Saviour but also as Lord and the one who has the right to direct and guide every aspect of our lives.
- a day when the church awakens out of its cosy, fireside comfort, to reach out into a cold world that needs to hear the Gospel, the Good News, and see the transforming change that comes to lives who accept Him on His terms
- a day when we see ourselves not just as believers but as disciples, walking in the footsteps of Jesus' life and ministry, whatever the cost.
- a day when people are talking of their personal need of Jesus and not denouncing and denying Him.

My first book, *Out of the Desert*, is centred on Exodus 32 and 33. There can be no forward movement without embracing God's challenge in these chapters. God was reminding Moses and Israel that living in the desert permanently was not His plan. God's promise given to

Moses in Exodus 6 gave him the courage to believe Him for deliverance from Pharaoh and slavery in Egypt. The Lord promised four things:

• I will bring you out from under the yoke of the Egyptians
• I will free you from being slaves
• I will redeem you with an outstretched arm and with mighty acts of judgment
• I will take you as my own people and I will be your God

Moses had already begun to experience these promises but he and the people of Israel were still in the desert. The desert was to be a very important training ground but God's intention was never for them, or us, to reside forever in that place.

I think it is important to remind ourselves of the central issue when we talk about God breaking through in today's world with power and authority. It is bringing the breath of revival but it is much more than ministry, increased activity and doing things for God.

When involved in ministry – at any level – our natural desire is always to see results, people responding and believing in Jesus. Why not? God's Word, according to Isaiah, is not to return to Him empty; it will accomplish what He desires for men, women and children. That is, to rescue them out of darkness and the grip of sin and Satan and experience the wonder of sins forgiven. Reconciliation with God enables us to receive the same Holy Spirit that Jesus received and to be adopted into His family, becoming an heir to all His Promises. However, the apostle Paul reminds us that the first move of the Spirit is not to use us but to change us, becoming God's aroma (2 Corinthians 2:15).

In Exodus 33 we see a critical challenge that both Moses and the people faced. We cannot proceed without getting past this point. God challenged them on three questions:

1. As He opens up the way toward the Promised Land of Canaan, will we be content with an angel leading us? In other words, do our hearts drift toward success at any cost even if God's Presence does not go with us?
2. How much do we desire His Presence and Glory? Does it have priority or would we sell it, like Esau, to satisfy our appetite for reputation, fame and fruitfulness?
3. How deep will our obedience be, especially in the tough times? Will we have a lifeboat in tow ready to jump ship when the storm rages?

The desert as a training ground
We have seen that to believe for exceptional times of unusual blessing will require us to look at our spiritual lives. This will cause us to examine ourselves with honesty and openness and to re-kindle that desperation to meet with Jesus in a new way. The personal need of transformation is our starting point, and this will sharpen our obedience no matter what challenges we face.

As many of us look back on our lives, we have perhaps struggled to understand (let alone embrace and profit from) our desert experiences. Some of us know people who are left bitter, discouraged or visionless by their deserts.

I remember some of my personal struggles. Going out to South-East Asia as a young, enthusiastic missionary my expectations were sky high. Thailand here I come, Buddhism – it is time to take a back seat, make way for Jesus!

11

<u>Learning the language</u> was for me a relatively positive experience, but with some crucial stages that had the potential to derail my missionary journey. The early fear of never being able to communicate in an effective and meaningful way was a daily barrier to cross. The many misunderstandings and miscommunications left me embarrassed, wondering if anyone would want to listen to me speak Thai again. The comparisons made with others who spoke so much better could easily have caused me to throw in the towel and revert to the safer ground of teaching English.

For many it can truly be a serious desert experience, especially when the language is tonal and very developed and intricate. You have so much you want to share, your testimony, the goodness of God that has changed your life, the tremendous truth of the Gospel and yet ... after an extended period of dedicated language learning, you can't even communicate effectively a simple phrase like 'Can I buy some toothpaste?'

I remember one young man from Alabama sent out by his church to Thailand. He was in my language class in Bangkok. His strong southern accent made it incredibly hard for him to pronounce the sounds and reproduce the tones of a delicate and beautiful Thai language. It was a desert experience that saw him return home to America feeling a total failure. Yes, the tears flow, some out of self-pity but others out of genuine compassion for those who have never heard and believed in Jesus as Saviour and Lord.

<u>Understanding the people</u>; for some strange reason I thought that everyone should think, act and respond like me. I had successfully negotiated all the cross cultural communication and cultural adjustment modules but the

root of pride is hard to remove. There is this tendency to think everyone should be like me, like us! I preferred to 'play host' in a country and situation where I am actually a 'guest'. When I began to discover the attitude changes that needed to take place it also transferred into a new spiritual path to 'walk humbly with God'. However, an enormous internal battle raged to keep me in the desert of my pride.

Sharing the Good News surely is straightforward, you just tell it as it is! In my early missionary training the Four Spiritual Laws booklet was all the rage. Maybe it had a measure of relevance in the United Kingdom at that time and in some parts of Asia, but I soon found out that this was not to be the case in Thailand. Sharing all my college notes, using all my best evangelistic sermons was like seed falling on hard ground. It left me crying out 'what's the point of being here?' and the small still voice replied 'it is primarily for you to change'.

Building the church, success at last, surely no more desert experiences? Wrong! I've learnt the language, understood the people, and developed a most Eastern approach to sharing the Good News. Having seen churches planted in more rural parts of north-west Thailand, now the church in Bangkok was beginning to grow numerically and in maturity. I've been a pastor in the United Kingdom so why not in Asia? It looks as if the sacrifice of leaving the home church is worthwhile after all.

Again pride quickly surges to pole position and that small voice whispers once more, 'pursue this path and you will never finish the race'. Why? Firstly, this church belongs to Jesus. Secondly, you are a guest in this land. You need to pass on the baton of leadership to those who belong to the host nation. Sound straightforward? Perhaps, but the internal battle that ensued became a significant desert experience.

<u>Overseeing church planting in many Asian countries</u>, surely you have reached the pinnacle of success in mission terms. Opportunities come to travel, speak and encourage church planting exploits in nine of the most significant nations in Asia. It is true, twenty-five years of mission experience enabled me to give advice, encouragement and direction, but I realised this was far less than God required. Supremely it is not about doing things for God, but God doing something new in me, in us. I was entering into a new desert experience, that of realising for all my activity and ministry, the well was running dry; it was time to change once again.

Woven into these desert places were times when I didn't understand what was going on. Why was God silent when I desperately needed to hear His voice? In the midst of a busy preaching and teaching schedule why am I struggling to get anything out of the Word of God? The more I desire to press on with God the greater seems to be the pull back into the old life. And the moments of failure, when I know I have disappointed God and people, where do I go from here? I feel lost and lonely. Sound familiar? Or is it only me?

The danger, when in the desert and tough periods of our lives, is to redefine God by our circumstances. When this happens the tendency is to ask the 'why' question. Why does God allow this? Why doesn't God come to my immediate rescue? Why, if God is all-loving, does He not demonstrate that to me now? Why has this happened to me, after all I have given up everything to serve Him? It just doesn't seem fair that I should have to go through this after all I have attempted to do and all the sacrifice I have made!

The Spirit of God graciously comes alongside us, and helps us to realise that whatever our circumstances may be, God never changes. Whether on the mountain top or in the deepest valley, we can discover the truth that with Him there is no variation or shadow of change (James 1:17).

In some situations He may come to us in wonderful forgiving love and at other times in holiness, demanding that we turn away from our sin, be cleansed, healed and restored. Regardless of how God may come to us, He is and always will be good. He is working all things for our good. Our circumstances cannot redefine God but become an opportunity for discovering and experiencing His unchanging nature and character, full of grace and truth.

> 'In him was life, and that life was the light of men. The light shines in the darkness, but the darkness has not understood or overcome it' (John 1:4-5)

This thought is paralleled clearly in the Old Testament. The prophet Isaiah speaks powerfully and puts things into perspective:

> *'A voice of one calling: in the desert place prepare the way for the Lord; make straight in the wilderness a highway for our God. Every valley shall be raised up, every mountain and hill made low; the rough ground shall become level, the rugged places a plain. And the glory of the Lord will be revealed and all mankind together will see it.'* (Isaiah 40:3-5)

Mark begins his gospel quoting this passage from Isaiah. John the Baptist is seen as the fulfilment of this Old Testament prophecy in preparation for the ministry of Jesus Christ. Jesus himself was led by the Spirit into the desert place, a place of physical danger and enormous spiritual temptation. It was from this desperate location and place of isolation that the Spirit of God was preparing Jesus to announce that the time has come. God's new day of revelation, redemption and reign had arrived, and man's first response should be to 'repent and believe.'

God's promise to Abram was to live in the land of Canaan. In the same way God's desire is that we enter into a new day of experiencing more of His awesome power, glory and holiness; His amazing grace and mercy leading us into victories of goodness over evil and the Kingdom of light over the kingdom of darkness. But at the same time it exposes us to the danger that perhaps lurking deep within us is a fleshly desire that requires instant pleasure, shallow happiness, artificial peace and shortcuts to success and fruitfulness; perhaps preferring an angel to the Presence of God as long as we succeed.

For you and me it is the reminder that Jesus is to be both Saviour and Lord. To seek Jesus and believe in Him provided there is no discomfort, inconvenience, pain and suffering may be a current preferred option in some places, but it has no part of God's new day.

China

My wife and I have had the privilege of going into China for many years. The church has so much to teach us. If ever a church experienced living in the desert, it was in China from 1949 to 1979, Mao Zedong's Great Leap Forward and the Cultural Revolution. This was an incredibly dark period where as many as thirty million Chinese, both Christians and non-Christian, lost their lives.

Many of the key pastors and leaders were imprisoned, some for between twenty and thirty years. All seemed lost and some newspapers in Asia even had the audacity to declare that God was now dead in China, the few remaining evangelicals being swallowed up in history. And yet with amazing courage, faith and sacrifice these desert times actually sharpened and enabled their spiritual lives to grow. For us we cannot imagine what these godly men and women endured for the sake of their faith. It was in these extreme times they discovered what they called 'prison theology' – basically that you will find out more about God in prison than anywhere else.

Yuan Xianchen was arrested in 1958 for refusing to join the Three Self Patriotic Movement, the official state church, because he opposed their theological modernism and believed that Jesus (and not a political group) was the head of the church. He was charged with being a counter-revolutionary and sentenced to life imprisonment. It was twenty-one years and eight months before he saw his wife and children again. He encouraged himself by singing 'The Old Rugged Cross' while the other prisoners had their smoking break. On release he went right back into having a house church.

The desert no longer paralysed them with fear but merely prepared them for fresh revelation and experience of God Himself.

It was in the darkest and most isolated desert experience that the vision for China was born. They wanted to share the Gospel to as many people as possible and to shape Chinese culture into Christ-like culture. Their Scriptural anchor was 1 Peter 4:12-13. *'Dear friends, do not be surprised at the painful trial you are suffering, as though something strange were happening to you. But rejoice that you participate in the sufferings of Christ, so that you may be overjoyed when his glory is revealed'.*
We finish this chapter with the encouragement of Isaiah ringing in our ears:

- Don't be afraid of the desert place
- God has not forsaken you or pushed you off into a cul-de-sac
- God is speaking comfort and strength into your heart
- Allow the Word and the Spirit to remove every obstacle, make the rough ground smooth, level the mountains and raise up the valleys
- God will turn the darkness into light
- Humble yourself in the tough place so that in due time, God's time, He may lift you up
- Lift up your voice; sing, sing!
- Be prepared to move on, out of the desert and into the land
- He will take hold of your right hand and help you; do not fear

Remember... the supreme privilege above all, far above fruitful ministry and worldly acclaim, is that of being in the Presence and Glory of the Lord. *'and the glory of the Lord will be revealed'* (Isaiah 40:5).

CHAPTER 3

Mercy and Grace

To get past the stiffest of tests, and humbly embrace the tough desert times, is nothing short of the mercy and grace of God in action. Sometimes the question is asked 'how did you manage to get through it all?' Whilst we may see this as an opportunity to put things down to our strength of character, dedicated resilience, perseverance and will-power, deep down we know it's not true. For myself I know that if it was left to me, the pressure of the moment, the subtle whisperings of Satan and the temptation of worldly acclaim, may tip the balance to make sure the spotlight is on me.

However, God displaying His goodness in all its fullness, as He did to Moses in Exodus 33:19, is an overwhelming declaration of His mercy and grace. Hebrews expresses this so well.

> 'Let us then approach the throne of grace with confidence, so that we may receive mercy and find grace to help us in our time of need' Hebrews 4:16

Only when the Spirit of God has deposited the wonder of mercy and grace afresh to our hearts, can we be ready for the next step of the journey with God.

Bathe afresh in the mercy of God

Mercy is a central aspect of God's character expressed in His desire to have a covenant relationship with undeserving people. Mercy is God's goodness confronting our misery and guilt. God's mercy is not simply a theological truth but was demonstrated in sending His Son. Mercy, then, leads into God's active compassion even to the point of sacrificing His life for us.

The prophet Micah directs our vision to God Himself. No one can compare with Him; He pardons and forgives sin and does not remain angry toward us but delights to show mercy.

> Micah 7:8, *'Do not gloat over me, my enemy! Though I have fallen, I will rise. Though I sit in darkness, the Lord will be my light'.*

There have been occasions when I have shown mercy because I felt it was expected of me as a Christian leader and missionary. It had a very hollow feel to it, and often the attitude behind the seemingly merciful action is one that is inwardly selfish and judgmental. That leaves your merciful act with little spiritual meaning. However, Micah takes us to God who absolutely delights in showing mercy; it pleases Him like nothing else. To receive it, we must first know that God is merciful.

> *'Praise be to the God and Father of our Lord Jesus Christ!
> In his great mercy he has given us new birth into a living
> hope through the resurrection of Jesus Christ from the dead,
> and into an inheritance that can never perish, spoil or fade —
> kept in heaven for you....'* 1 Peter 1:3-4

From dying in the gutter to the throne of God's mercy.

In the last few years Wilma and I have had the privilege
of serving with WEC Betel, a church planting mission
organisation working worldwide to rescue broken and
addicted lives. The most amazing moments come when a
broken, defeated drug or alcohol addict is suddenly made
aware by the Spirit of God that no matter how devastating
and dark his or her situation may be, God's mercy goes
further. Some have been judged by their parents, family,
neighbourhood, society and even the church, discarded to
the street gutter or the rubbish tip.

Dhaka, Bangladesh

I still have a vivid memory of walking into a desperate
drug area of Dhaka. So many families crammed into such
an incredibly small area. The squalor and stench of urine
flowing in the gutters between the shanty homes took my
breath away. The sight of small children, with barely a
piece of cloth on them, playing in this infested and diseased
environment was sickening. It was a dangerous area for a
foreigner to be and I thought that this is the nearest to a
living hell that I have been in. I found myself thinking
that this is not a place for a missionary to be — surely there
is no hope here. And yet to my astonishment the God of

mercy had begun to break into this desperate community. I had the privilege of meeting two Bangladeshi Christian brothers who literally ran a rescue shop within a yard of this earthly hell. Yes, we can so easily judge but God's mercy travels further than judgment.

Charles Finney

Oct. 10th 1821 while praying alone in the woods outside his village, Finney experienced a powerful conversion. That evening in his small office he had a vision that he fell weeping at Jesus' feet.

'I received a mighty baptism of the Holy Ghost.....without expecting it, without ever having the thought in my mind that there was such a thing for me, without any recollection that I have ever heard the thing being mentioned by any person in the world, at a moment entirely unexpected by me, the Holy Spirit descended upon me in a manner that seemed to go through me, body and soul'.

Few men have experienced the refining power of the Spirit more than Finney. Years later in August 1825 Finney travelled to central New York. After preaching the first time he had a real burden to pray. The following Sunday God came in power at the church services and he met a Mrs Harris who had wrestled in prayer day and night, she said:

'The Lord has come; this work will spread over this entire region. A cloud of mercy overhangs us all and we shall see such a work of grace as we have never yet seen.'

The fire of God's Spirit began to burn. People began to weep and cry unable to control their feelings. When

Finney visited their homes some could only kneel or prostrate themselves on the floor. Many were convicted by the Word and overwhelmed by the Spirit. Revival services went on for 20 nights; all were amazed at how many were converted.

The sheriff of Utica, some twenty miles away, came on business and laughed and mocked the revival. But suddenly an awesome feeling of the presence of God gripped him. He found the business establishments so overcome with awe for God that they could hardly speak. He too was soon converted!

Finney urged the people to pray to God earnestly and expectantly for the immediate outpouring of the Spirit. Soon the town was full of prayer.

I love those words: "a cloud of mercy overhangs us all and we shall see such a work of grace as we have never yet seen"

As I have talked with leaders of Betel in India (known as Asha Bhawan — meaning House of Hope) their desperate past has enabled them to grasp the truth of God's mercy to a depth and wonder I had previously never appreciated. The Holy Spirit illuminated my heart to see that though my past had never reached the depth of many of my ex-drug and alcoholic friends, it was the same mercy of God that gave me the chance of experiencing grace.

No matter how theologically trained we may be, there is the temptation to believe that we are worthy of God's mercy — certainly more so than the drug addicts. I learned that it is not my ex-drug and alcoholic friends alone but I too that have been raised from the gutter to the throne of God's mercy and grace.

God's judgment has been satisfied in the death of Jesus upon the Cross. Jesus took upon Himself our sin so that we can receive mercy and find grace. We come to God in our chains, and mercy meets us head on; we leave with that chorus resounding from an ever-grateful heart, 'my chains are gone, I've been set free'.

Be in awe of the grace of God

As mercy is God's goodness confronting our misery and guilt, so grace is His goodness giving to us the benefit of heaven's wonder and glory, even though we are so undeserving. Grace enables us to lift our heads and exchange our prison cell and rags for the royal robes of His righteousness and His presence.

This is beautifully shown in Luke 15:11-24 and the story of the Prodigal Son, or rather the Father's love. The love and grace of God is freely available for our broken world. He has not turned His back on us, but waits patiently for us to respond and return. Grace sends out a clear message, 'I am here for you. I am looking out for your return. I am ready to receive you, for now is the time to receive forgiveness and the healing love of God, and to be set free'.

Down through the centuries the grace of God has transformed lives. William Bengo Collyer (1782-1854) wrote these stunning words:

> 'Return, O wanderer, now return,
> And seek the Father's face;
> Those new desires which in thee burn

Were kindled by His grace.
Return, O wanderer, now return,
And wipe the falling tear:
The Father calls, no longer mourn;
'Tis love invites thee near'

'But because of his great love for us, God who is rich in mercy, made us alive with Christ even when we were dead in transgressions — it is by grace you have been saved.' Ephesians 2:4

The truth is that mercy and grace have no beginning and no end because they are central to God's character. The Old Testament and the New Testament bear witness to the mercy and grace of God in so many ways. Without mercy and grace there would have been no Abraham, friend of God. Gideon would never have become a mighty warrior. David most certainly would have not been called a man after God's own heart. Hebrews chapter eleven has inspired so many and yet without mercy and grace this chapter would not have been written. In the mission world Peter and Paul are wonderful, inspiring examples of men doing amazing exploits for God, but only the mercy and grace of God made that possible.

At a time when many are sensing that God is about to move, bringing in His new day, it is not surprising that mercy and grace become centre stage. They are resurrected from being set in cold concrete theological pillars. The fire of God's Spirit illuminates the mercy and grace of God afresh to us, pumping new wonder, awe and hope into bodies that are sagging under the weight of failure and fruitlessness, world oppression and evil.

It was no different for Moses and Israel. From this position God was about to announce something of great importance and now he speaks to us too. When mercy and grace have been ministered to our hearts by the Spirit of God, we are in a position to receive His next command.

CHAPTER 4

Be Ready

Exodus 34:2, *'Be ready in the morning, and then come up on Mount Sinai.'*

When I read this verse it became for me a very personal and prophetic moment. I use the word prophetic in the sense that God opened heaven a little bit to enable me to see and hear what is on His heart.

As we prepare to move out of the desert and into the land, it is impossible for us to work out this God-given journey and mission without hearing clearly from Father. Without God's prophetic voice speaking to us, the danger is that we will always be reacting to situations rather than being proactive and moving in step with the Spirit. And we will always look for the comfortable middle ground rather than living on the edge of impossibility. To live on the edge of impossibility can be relegated to the eccentric few but I wonder if God views it like this? I do not think so. Perhaps it is more likely He would say, 'This is normal Christianity and the walk of faith'.

Paul tells the Corinthian church in chapter fourteen that the prophetic word will comfort, encourage, strengthen and edify. Some of the notable writers like Bruce and

Tozer amplify this in a helpful way. They say it is sensing, hearing and seeing what is on the mind of God for a current situation. And when this happens it has the ability to comfort, strengthen and encourage, but also to:

alarm, just imagine meeting with God in the cloud of His Presence;

to move us, as a multitude of emotions flood in of both fear and extraordinary favour; and

to challenge. This is what you would expect when God speaks to a particular people at a particular moment; you can't stand still but know it is time to move on.

In addition to this, prophecy conveys vision and purpose to God's people. The Holy Spirit opens our eyes to see the wonder of the true meaning and purpose of life. He enables us to see beyond our natural eyesight and walk by faith. He reveals to us what the church is meant to be. He shows us what we are supposed to become as we enter the land, and the centrality of the mission heart of God. Thus he helps us to refuse to settle for the convenient, comfortable and the respectable that keeps us pleasing man rather than God.

Prophecy calls us back to the Word of God, and not to water down the Gospel. It challenges us to marry the Word of God with the anointing of the Spirit.

It is hard to believe that Moses got a good sleep that night. Hours of sweating, tossing and turning, wondering if he will survive this moment. Later, Malachi wrote in chapter 3:2-3, 'Who can stand when he appears? For he will be like a refiner's fire.'

The reason God's word to Moses came with such prophetic impact to me was to counter the idea that some in the past have brought, saying, 'If God wants to bring in a new day He will and there is nothing we can do about it.'

There is an element of truth in this statement but also an element that needs to be challenged. Let's look at both now.

<u>Sovereignty of God:</u>
The element of truth is that behind every new day and move of God's Spirit there is the hallmark of divine sovereignty. This means that God rules His entire creation, and to be sovereign He must be all-knowing, all-powerful and free to do whatever He wants. The coming of the Holy Spirit at Pentecost well illustrates the sovereignty of God in His timing and fulfilment of prophecy. It was not a last minute decision on the part of God to pour out the Holy Spirit in Acts 2. Its meaning and background goes right back into the Old Testament, to Exodus 34:22.

'Celebrate the Feast of Weeks with the first fruits of the wheat harvest, and the Feast of Ingathering at the turn of the year.'

Pentecost was called the Feast of Weeks and also the Feast of Harvest because on that day the people presented to the Lord the first fruits of the annual wheat harvest, the harvest festival. In Greek Pentecost means 'fiftieth' and marked this annual Jewish festival scheduled fifty days after the Passover.

The harvest theme was also prophetic. It looked forward to a coming day when the Holy Spirit would be poured out on broken lives, causing them to be reconciled to God, birthing a spiritual harvest. The Old Testament prophets spoke about this day:

Ezekiel 36:26, 27 'I will give you a new heart; I will put a new spirit in you; I will put My Spirit in you and cause you to move ...'

Isaiah 44:3 'I will pour water on thirsty ground and streams on dry ground; I will pour out My Spirit on your offspring and blessing on your descendants.'

Joel 2:28, 29 'I will pour out My Spirit on all people, sons and daughters, young men, old men, servants men and women.'

Isaiah tells us that the Spirit's coming is to empower the life and ministry of the Messiah. The anointing would enable Jesus to preach the Word of God powerfully and with conviction, to bind up broken lives, to free captive slaves, to release from the darkness and grip of Satan, proclaiming that the year of the Lord's favour had come. Supremely the Spirit would lead Jesus to Calvary, the apex of his ministry.

When we look at Calvary, its timing and events, we see God's sovereign hand so clearly. The law was given on Mount Sinai on the fiftieth day after the Passover lamb was killed. The lamb was killed at three o'clock in the afternoon. On the third day after the Passover, the slaves were set free. Now as we pick things up in the New Testament, Jesus died at three o'clock in the afternoon, the very time when thousands of Passover lambs were being slaughtered. No wonder that the Spirit caused John the Baptist to cry out:

John 1:29 'Look, the Lamb of God who takes away the sin of the world.'

Jesus, after three days, rose from the dead; the last enemy had been conquered. For forty days, Acts 1:3 tells us, Jesus taught on the Kingdom of God. After His ascension the disciples were in the upper room for a further ten days. Total this up and it comes to fifty days. God's time had come, the heavens opened and the Spirit came. There was nothing random and last minute with God's preparation and timing. Jesus was born at just the right time (Galatians 4:4) at the Father's appointed time. Jesus died at the Father's appointed time (Acts 2:22,23). Jesus rose from the dead at the Father's appointed time (Acts 2:24). The Holy Spirit came at the Father's appointed time; Pentecost was orchestrated by God Himself.

The impact and victory of the Cross would bring both present and eternal comfort to those who repent and believe, but also a transformed heart made completely new, filled with praise and thanksgiving. This spirit of joy takes away the spirit of despair. But above all, the coming of the Spirit will not point to the accomplishment of man but display His splendour and His glory.

Jesus had declared in John 4:35, 36 and Matthew 9:37,38 that the harvest is plentiful. And now the same Spirit that Jesus received came upon the one hundred and twenty disciples. Later, Paul writing to the Romans in chapter eight emphasises this truth. It was to impart and empower them to carry the gospel of the Kingdom to the ends of the earth. Yes, to be God's labourers in His worldwide harvest field.

Jesus had come to save the lost and now it was God's intent to marshal, discipline, strengthen and multiply His Church until all the peoples on earth have had a chance to hear the gospel unobstructed by cultural and linguistic barriers.

When it comes to God's new day whether past, present or future, Paul makes it clear that only God can makes things happen.

> 'I planted the seed, Apollos watered it, but God made it grow.' 1 Corinthians 3:6

The spiritual readiness of man

The element to be challenged is that we can do nothing about it. It seems to me that God's new day has two sides to it: the divine sovereignty of God and the spiritual readiness of man. When Paul mentions that God uses the foolish things of the world to confound the wise, it merely reinforces to us that the people He uses are often very surprising but, as we shall see, they are ready for God.

James McQuilkin came from the parish of Connor about five miles from Ballymena in Northern Ireland. He worked in a linen warehouse in the town. He was known in the village as the man who reared fighting cocks. Cockfighting was a blood sport in which roosters were placed in a ring and forced to fight to the death for amusement and profit; it is now illegal. However, in 1856 an English lady by the name of Mrs Colville came to Ballymena. She began to go from house to house with a view to leading people to a personal faith in Christ.

Less than a year later she returned to England discouraged, believing that her time in Ireland had been unfruitful. But it was not true. Just before she left she visited Miss Brown. Two other ladies and James McQuilkin were present at that meeting. She spoke about the importance of seeking a personal faith in Jesus and the need of the new birth.

James was deeply touched by the Spirit of God and a short

time afterwards he came to a saving knowledge of Christ. So here we have a normal, unknown, dedicated Christian lady used by God in the conversion of James McQuilkin, who was to become one of the most significant figures in the 1859 revival in Ulster.

However, it is something that James said that God used to challenge me. And in fact this began a personal quest to be prepared for God's surprises.

'If God has visited His people before, why not again?'

We could add to that, if God used an ordinary, unknown, dedicated Christian woman like Mrs. Colville, why not us? If God could prepare the heart of James McQuilkin, why not you or me?

The question remains, do we have no part?

We can listen to the hyper-Calvinist who says 'leave it all to God' or to the hyper-Arminian who says 'it is all up to us'. This can leave us confused, stuck in neutral gear going nowhere. As we see from revival history God used men and women from both theological camps. Wesley, Whitefield and Finney may not have agreed on certain issues, but there is no question that God looked beyond that and saw hearts desperate, longing, passionate and ready to be changed at whatever personal cost. Their hearts were set on being in the manifest presence of a holy God, whose love, power, mercy and grace would turn lives upside down and bring salvation to the lost.

How we would love to read on the front page of today's tabloids the impact that revival has had on society over the centuries:

- revival closes the shops
- a large flourishing high school run by a sceptic principal sees many of the students weeping over their sin (nearly 40 of whom later became missionaries.)
- at harvest time farmers leave their fields to attend a midday church revival service
- a spirit of prayer grips the nation; ten thousand groups meet for prayer at midday. Businesses put up signs 'closed; will open at the end of the prayer meeting'
- people give their lives to Christ in homes, shops, fields and churches

James McQuilkin would challenge us 'why not today?'

God may not do things the same way as yesterday; it may not be a few great preachers that get the headlines. What about the power of unity within the churches? Why not the resurrection power of the Spirit of Christ breathing new life and power through the Universities' Christian Unions? God is no respecter of age or gender. You may be a young man, twenty-two year old like Whitefield or eighty-two and eighty-four year old like Christine and Peggy Smith, one bent double with arthritis and the other blind, used by God in the 1949-52 Hebridean Revival. No-one is surplus to God's requirements.

Foundational to preparing our hearts is the belief that God has not finished with displaying His mighty power, no matter how dark today's world may seem.

In Matthew 9:28 Jesus asks the blind man a straight question: 'Do you believe that I am able to do this?' and I wonder if He is not asking us the same question concerning His harvest. Later on in verses 37-38 Jesus says:

'The harvest is plentiful but the workers are few. Ask

the Lord of the harvest, therefore, to send out workers into His harvest field.'

Surely, if we are asking the Lord of the harvest to pour out His Spirit and mobilise his workers, it seems to me that we have a responsibility to get ready, as we may be part of the answer.

Psalm 44:1, 'We have heard it with our ears O God; our ancestors have told us what you did in their days, in days long ago.' James McQuilkin could not let this scripture pass him by without his heart replying, 'Lord, you can do that again.'

This new day is determined by God alone, and emphasizes His sovereignty. After all, He is the Alpha and Omega, the beginning and the end; but in that day some of His people have met the conditions by being ready and willing, which reveals the aspect of spiritual preparation.

Jesus promises us that He is coming back, but does not disclose the date or hour. Yet He calls on us to be ready and not to be caught by surprise but watch for the signs of His return. Isn't this the case with revival? We do not know the date on which it will come or the places it will touch. John tells us there is a mystery to the wind of the Spirit, and we are to be ready for the unexpected.

John 3:8, 'The wind blows wherever it pleases. You hear its sound, but you cannot tell where it comes from or where it is going. So it is with everyone born of the Spirit'.

Reflection point as we review this chapter. How does this impact you and me? Are we ready? Are we available? Are we willing to be changed, shaped and prepared? Is there an urgency, a sense of imminence, and awareness of God's now? Would a visitation from God take us by surprise? Would God have to search elsewhere for a suitable instrument?

CHAPTER 5

In the morning

Exodus 34:2-3, *'Be ready in the morning to come up Mount Sinai... present yourself to me there on the top of the mountain... no-one is to come with you'.*

I have always preferred to be on time or even early for appointments, even the dentist! When it comes to flying, I plan to be at the airport at least three hours before take-off; ready and prepared for any last minute adjustments that may need to be made and priming myself for the coming journey.

In my early missionary days in north-west Thailand, working among mostly rural people, my preference for punctuality was seriously challenged. In those days few farmers had watches and the sun and its position told their time. As the number of small, seeker and home groups grew, meetings were arranged for most days of the week. Cloudy and overcast weekday meetings rarely started on time, with often a delay of an hour or more. For the farmers this was no problem, but I confess I struggled. I tried to smile and appear in control of my emotions because that's very important in the Thai Buddhist context. However, deep inside I was far from happy. I felt sorry for myself, having to sit around waiting for a meeting to begin which should have finished by now.

As I was reflecting on this more recently, I realised that secondary to punctuality was the readiness of my heart and my preparation for meeting with God, and even the thought of a new visitation. It was more 'some time' than 'in the morning'. In the same way that the overcast conditions made it difficult for the Thai farmer to guess the time of day, so my busyness and ministry duties had dulled my spiritual senses.

Chronos and *Kairos*

In the New Testament, the Greek words *chronos* and *kairos* both mean time.

Chronos refers to the duration of time like a season, winter, spring, summer and harvest. It can also mean a span of time, so many hours, minutes and seconds. As I waited for the farmers to be ready for the meeting, I had a *chronos* perspective counting the hours, minutes and seconds for everyone to be ready.

Kairos on the other hand adds a new dimension of meaning. It sees a moment in time, not simply as hours, minutes and seconds, but when God advances His purposes. As the sovereign God He stands outside time and space as its Creator and inside time and space as its Redeemer. In that moment it is my responsibility to be aware of what the Spirit is doing and to give God the opportunity to advance His purpose now, in this moment of time.

I was learning a lesson about being ready in the morning. This is a mindset change and a personal challenge. Whilst being a good steward of God's *chronos* moments is right and good, for example my involvement in mission activity,

I can still be oblivious to immediate things that are on God's heart. The Spirit needed to attune my heart to God's *kairos* opportunities and 'now' breakthrough. If you excuse the pun, I must be a watchman!

What is the lesson? 'Don't let your diligence toward *chronos* block your awareness of God's *kairos* moment.'

Deut.11:13, 14, 'So if you faithfully obey the commands I am giving to you today – to love the Lord your God and to serve Him with all your heart and with all your soul – then I will send rain on your land in its season, both autumn and spring rains, so that you may gather in your grain, new wine and oil'.

<u>What does the 'morning' represent?</u>
The word morning is found extensively in the Bible. It occurs more than 200 times in the Old Testament alone. Although the term 'morning' is somewhat imprecise in the Bible, it carries several important meanings.

The morning can be seen to be of particular importance both as a time for beginning the normal activities and duties of life, and as a special time for spiritual commitment and encounter. Together, they symbolise the start of a new and ever-increasing awareness and experience concerning all that God desires to do in our lives and in the world.

In both cases, morning is God's special time, and it represents human opportunity to achieve something purposeful and to meet with God in a new way. In contrast to the evening, the morning is associated with divine activity, fresh light, truth, revelation and care.

This divine activity can be seen in many varied ways. Moses and the people of Israel had already experienced this in Exodus 16:6, 12, 13, 21 as manna was provided every morning. In contrast, Zephaniah affirms that every morning God reveals his justice (Zeph. 3:5). With the light of each day his justice was revealed to his people in kindly acts, or in warnings through his prophets for the need of spiritual change. So the morning can have a positive and more negative idea, but the greater significance is that of meeting with God in a new way and spiritual transformation.

In Exodus 34:2 the morning brings this sense of God about to meet Moses in a new personal way. This, as we have seen, is not only an opportunity to recall God's mercy and grace, but also to prepare for a fresh experience of his abundant faithfulness, leading to a new beginning and a future hope.

Lamentations 3:21-23

'Yet this I call to mind and therefore have hope: Because of the Lord's great love we are not consumed, for his compassions never fail. They are new every morning; great is your faithfulness.'

Lamentations was written by the prophet Jeremiah alongside the book of Jeremiah. Jeremiah is weeping over the nation, and through the gloom and doom God speaks some powerful, prophetic and encouraging words. No more so than in Jeremiah 18 and the illustration at the potter's house. The potter's intention was to make a beautiful pot. The problem was the clay. Because of the condition of the clay the potter couldn't make the pot he originally intended.

The prophetic word became clear. God was saying that it is not too late, and through repentance and genuine change we can still become the beautiful pot He intended.

This is brought out in Lamentations 3:21-23. The different translations combine to point us to the newness of every morning. God's amazing love has not run out, there is still so much more to understand and to receive. God's mercy and compassion have not dried up, they spring up from an everlasting fountain of goodness. God's faithfulness has not been exhausted by our unfaithfulness. Every morning new measures of His love, mercy, compassion and faithfulness are available to be received. No wonder Jeremiah underpins all of this by saying that when he reflects upon this, he has hope (verse 21.)

I want to grasp hold of this hope Jeremiah speaks about. The future is not determined by the past but by engaging with God in the present. Many have a burden for this nation. The tears are flowing just as they did through Jeremiah. Encouragement comes from believing that in this difficult and dark moment God is giving us a new morning moment of His amazing grace.

Someone said that God is a God of a thousand new beginnings. When we look at our own lives, we may be tempted to think we have already used them up. But Lamentations 3:21-23 proves us wrong! As I look at today's world, the church and my personal life and also reflect back to the time of Moses and Exodus 34, four things about a new morning become clear: renewal, hope, revelation and discovery.

A new morning of renewal and hope

Putting it very simply, renewal is the transformation by God of the lives of His people. This can be individual and corporate. Hope is that confident expectation of God's promised blessings; ultimately an inheritance that is eternal, forever living in the presence of God.

Renewal is so much part of our Christian vocabulary there is a danger that we can dismiss it as ordinary and not a big deal; however to do so would be tragic and untimely especially as we think about God's new day. As a new Christian I remember travelling up to London to attend lectures of the Fountain Trust, founded to promote charismatic renewal. I learned that renewal was not a minor tweak but a transforming moment. It was an encounter with the Holy Spirit as in Acts 2.

So what will renewal 'in the morning' look like?

I need to remind myself that renewal is not revival, but the point from which our hearts are stirred to pray for revival and to receive more of the Spirit.

There was a theological depth shared at those London lectures which has stayed with me to this day. Whilst we rejoice when the Spirit makes our spiritual lives fresh and strong again, filled with more passion and purpose, regenerated and revived, hungry for the Word of God, it does not finish there. The Holy Spirit's supreme work is to bring us to Christ and to minister Christ in all His fullness. In the mystery of the Godhead the Holy Spirit's entire ministry is to glorify the Father and the Son.

John 16:13-15

'But when he, the Spirit of truth comes, he will guide you into all truth. He will not speak on his own; he will speak only what he hears, and he will tell you what is to come. He will bring glory to me by taking from what is mine and making it known to you. All that belongs to the Father is mine. That is why I said the Spirit will take from what is mine and make it known to you'.

Morning renewal will lead us into the presence and glory

of Christ. What I mean by glory is the revealed person, character, work and power of the Lord Jesus Christ. And in that new morning of renewal and encounter, our eyes will be opened to see more clearly the magnificence of Jesus and to rediscover what the confession 'Jesus is Lord' (1 Corinthians 12:3) really means.

A new morning of revelation and discovery

After nearly forty years of being a missionary in Asia, one of my ongoing personal challenges is the truth that I am not as spiritual as I think I am. Spiritual maturity can be cloaked and cosmetically brushed up in so many ways.

In Thailand, looking the part is very important. The assumption is that if you wear a suit, tie, and drive a nice car you must be successful, someone to be admired. Because of appearance you may be addressed as 'Aajarn' a term of respect meaning an educated teacher or one from whom others can learn. This may truly be the case but maybe not, the appearance simply covering an unseen bankrupt or corrupt lifestyle.

Over the last years the Spirit of God has been working in me in the same way. What is spiritual maturity? I can pass it off in many ways:

- Forty years serving Jesus
- A reasonable knowledge of the Word and two theological degrees to prove it
- I gave up my accountancy career, and travelled outside my comfort zone to live in Asia
- I've seen Buddhist people come to faith in Jesus
- I've seen rural churches in north-west Thailand, and a church in Bangkok come into being
- Together with my wife Wilma, we have seen our

children grow up in Asia, become Christians and return to the United Kingdom for university, and now married with Christian family life-styles
• I've overseen church planting in nine countries in South-East Asia

The list could go on, and in times of justifying myself before God I have done just that. There may be elements here that do point to a measure of maturity, but when God is calling me to His new day, there is no hiding from the penetrating light of the Spirit; my mask of self-righteousness must come off.

Christian maturity does not automatically come with age. Grey hairs in Asia do open doors of ministry, people assuming that with age comes maturity. They can be right but also so awfully wrong.

Spiritual maturity does not appear with one flash of revelation. Hebrews 6:1 'Let us go on to maturity,' and the clear sense of the verb is to continue progressing toward this goal.

Possessing spiritual gifts, important though they are, cannot be equated with maturity. Paul's exhortations to the Corinthian church make this clear.

1 Corinthians 1:7, 'Therefore you do not lack any spiritual gift as you eagerly wait for our Lord Jesus to be revealed.'

1 Corinthians 3:1-3a, 'Brothers do not address yourselves as spiritual but as worldly – mere infants in Christ. I gave you milk, not solid food, for you were not ready for it. Indeed you are still not ready. You are still worldly ...'

Spiritual maturity is being like Christ. We are as mature as our lives reflect the life of Christ. Wonderful though this increased revelation and discovery of who Jesus is, it will also be painful to realise just how far we are from His likeness.

Ephesians 4:11-13, 'It was he who gave some to be apostles, some to be prophets, some to be evangelists, and some to be pastors and teachers, to prepare God's people for works of service, so that the body of Christ may be built up, until we all reach unity in the faith and in the knowledge of the Son of God and become mature, attaining to the whole measure of the fullness of Christ'.

God's purpose is to produce disciples who fulfil their humanity and become what He designed them to be. There will be an ever increasing transformation as Paul tells us in 2 Corinthians 3:18, but there will also be a final transformation moment as John reveals to us.

1 John 3:2, 3, 'Dear friends, now we are children of God, and what we will be has not yet been made known. But we know that when he appears, we shall be like him, for we shall see him as he is. Everyone who has this hope in Him purifies himself, just as he is pure.'

What is the point for Moses and us?

Moses himself was not a stranger to revelation and discovery. God had already broken through revealing Himself as the 'I AM' (Exodus 3:14). Various attempts have been made to explain its significance, but in the simplest form it seems to be a promise of God's faithful presence with his people. He would not fail Israel in any of His promises. Nothing could hinder Him in His faithfulness because He is all-powerful.

In Exodus 6 we have already mentioned about God's Covenant of redemption from slavery and His promise to bring them into the land. Exodus 16:6-7 'in the evening you will know that it was the Lord who brought you out of Egypt, and in the morning you will see the glory of the Lord.' Here there is a fresh discovery, through the provision of manna, that the I AM who rescued them from Egypt will also be faithful day by day just as He promised.

You and I could similarly recall and marvel at God's revelation to us over the years, and when we do so they become moments that awaken us out of our night's sleep and prepare us for the new morning.

I believe the work of the Holy Spirit is to put upon our hearts the cry of John 12:21, 'we would like to see Jesus'. The revelation and discovery of God's new morning will be centred on the person of Jesus. Just as maturity is not about what I do or have done, but the measure to which my life in word and deed reflects the life of Christ.

Over the centuries God has opened up heaven and sent revival and the exaltation of Jesus has and always will be centre stage.

The growth and expansion of Asha Bhawan in Asia has been an amazing, supernatural journey. Begun by Keith and Lolita Bergmeier, Betel leaders from Australia and Mexico, it has expanded into 14 cities and 10 States in India plus Nepal and Mongolia and this has been breathtaking. There is a hunger among many for God's new day. In Gurgaon, the main centre of Asha Bhawan in the Harayana State of north India, inscribed on the lectern in the worship auditorium are the words from John 12:21 'we would see Jesus'. This above everything else sums up the new morning.

The Word of God makes that clear. Jesus is to be my Saviour, Lord, my Master and King, the Christ, the Anointed One, the Messiah, the Son of the living God, the Alpha and Omega, the Beginning and the End, the Author and Finisher of our faith, the Vine, the Bread of Life, the Water of Life, the Way, the Truth and the Life, the only gate, the Good Shepherd, the Lily of the Valley, the Fairest of Ten Thousand, the Word of God, the I AM; for He is the image of the invisible God, the Ruler of all Creation, the Firstborn from the dead, the King of kings, and the Lord of lords, the One who holds all things together by his powerful word. He is to be Jesus, my Jesus, and the One who alone is worthy of praise.

Exodus 34:10, 11
Then the Lord said: 'I am making a covenant with you. Before all your people I will do wonders never before done in any nation in all the world. The people you live among will see how awesome is the work that I, the Lord, will do for you. Obey what I command you today. I will drive out before you the Amorites, Canaanites, Hittites, Perizzites, Hivites and Jebusites.'

James McQuilkin would challenge us 'why not today?'

CHAPTER 6

Why does God ask us to present ourselves to Him?

Part one

Exodus 34:2-3, *'Be ready in the morning to come up Mount Sinai ... present yourself to me there on the top of the mountain ... no-one is to come with you'.*

For Moses, the leader, it is a special God given moment to attune his heart to God's heart. For Israel it is a moment to realise the overflowing and undeserved mercy and grace of God toward them. Despite their sin and rebellion, He has not forsaken them, and His covenantal promise will be fulfilled to them and through them. For Israel, entering Canaan represented so many victories waiting to take place with God as commander of the army. When they move forward in obedience, then He will display His almighty power. The enemies of God and His Kingdom will be gloriously defeated, and His people will enter into their inheritance.

For us this is echoed in the New Testament.

As a Christian leader I am to see the importance of this *kairos* moment, a fresh meeting with Jesus. The words in Revelation ring loud and clear at such a moment: 'He who has an ear, let him hear what the Spirit is saying.' The same oneness that Jesus has with the Father is his goal for us too; it is time to attune and align our heart to God's heart.

For us in the church, God's people and family, it is the moment not to wallow in self-pity and godlessness, but to be bathed afresh in the love of God and His overflowing and undeserved mercy and grace. To rejoice in the truth that He has not forsaken us, and His promises to us, complete in Jesus, will be fulfilled through us to the Father's glory.

Mission is often such a lonely and forgotten journey. The way ahead and entrance into the land represents the final thrust to reach the unreached and fulfil the Great Commission. This worldwide commission given by Jesus to His disciples has not been pushed aside, but is still firmly in place and at the centre of God's heart and agenda.

And so the Old Testament and the New Testament harmonise.

Psalm 2:8, 'Ask of me and I will make the nations your inheritance, the ends of the earth your possession.'

Acts 1:8, 'But you will receive power when the Holy Spirit comes upon you; and you will be my witnesses in Jerusalem, Judea, Samaria and to the ends of the earth.'

There is a subtle danger at this moment. We can feel the excitement rising. The revelation that God has not forsaken us, but is still fully committed as ever, gives us fresh strength and courage. The realisation that we are still important and significant in the fulfilling of His plans makes us feel ten feet tall and world-beaters. The genuine desire to be part of world mission that finishes the task given in Matthew 28:18-20 makes every other vision, goal and objective seem unimportant. It inspires us like nothing else. Just imagine being part of that final move of taking the gospel to every tribe, tongue and nation! I cannot think of anything better than to hear the Father's voice: 'Well done, good and faithful servant, job done, mission accomplished, it's time to come Home!'

Where is the danger then?

Simply this: the temptation at this point is for the ministry, vision, and action part of me to go into overdrive. Having had a privileged glimpse of what the future may hold and God's new day promises, that old familiar voice inside me says, 'you can do it'. I get to work and resurrect my plans and goals, and lay out my strategy as to how I can make this all happen.

Having had the privilege of being a pastor in the United Kingdom as well as a missionary establishing and supervising church plants across Asia, I know that this challenge affects most leaders, me included. From my own life, as well as many other missionaries, a pattern often emerges.

Stage 1

When the going is really tough and unresponsive, we are totally at a loss as to what to do and how to do it. The result is that we earnestly seek God for His answer.

I had just finished my first phase of language learning in Bangkok and now had been placed in Sukhothai, the ancient capital of Thailand. I was desperate to lead people to a personal faith in Christ. Feeling totally ill-equipped I decided to have three days prayer and fasting at a very basic camp at the top of a mountain outside Chiangmai. I had just water to drink. No other person was staying in the huts, and my only company were the night-time rats chewing at the bed in which I was trying to sleep. However, my mind was focussed. I needed to get close to God, hear His voice, and trust the Spirit of God to do what I could not do, namely, open the eyes of the blind to see their need of Jesus.

Stage 2

This is when God graciously answers and shows us the way forward. Out of this comes fruit, which is so encouraging. People come to faith.

This is what I experienced. On return to Sukhothai I was unaware that the Holy Spirit was already at work in the lives of two young men. He made sure I met up with them in the market, and we became friends. The initial interest was probably in me as a foreigner, and secondly their wanting to learn English; they would use it to earn money driving foreigners in their three-wheeled vehicles to the ancient Buddhist ruins in the old city. However, it became deeper than that, and both came to a personal faith in Jesus. One later became an elder in the church.

Stage 3

Believers become disciples and get involved in the expansion and growth of the church. So now I know how to build church; after all it is happening in front of my eyes. The latest discipleship course and church planting methods from around the world become very appealing. I too want to see the church grow rapidly. My keenness to see results and import the latest way of seeing church grow may have had the right motive, but was directed by my initiative and not always by the Spirit of God.

Whilst reflecting on these three stages I realised how easily this repeating pattern emerges in ministry:

- In desperation seek God totally
- In fruitfulness seek God as is necessary
- In desperation seek God totally
- In fruitfulness seek God as is necessary

If that appears harsh and judgmental it is not meant to be. It simply highlights that our focus on results can distract us from seeing our desperate need of a fresh encounter with God and an outpouring of the Spirit. God asks a very straight question in Acts 7:49: 'What kind of house will you build for me?' He has already made it clear that He does not live in houses made by men. Our immediate response is that we are building God's house, and yet when the Spirit shines His searching light on our ministry, perhaps there is too much sand and not enough rock! The reason why God commands us to present ourselves before Him must surely centre on the fact that He wants His work done His way and me to be more like Him.

God has a pattern

The truth so clearly displayed through the Old and the New Testament is that God has a pattern or blueprint. The glory of God only descends according to the divine pattern or way of doing things. As someone said, neither a heap of stones nor a pile of materials on a piece of land is a house. All must be assembled and built according to the plan of the Architect.

God had already made this point clear to Noah with the building of the Ark. Noah built the Ark according to the design given to him by God. Genesis 6:22, 'Noah did everything just as God commanded'.

The sacrificial altars (Exodus 20:24-26) were also to be made according to God's commands. No tool was to be used to shape the stones, unlike heathen altars made by human hands. To approach and worship God must be done God's way.

The details of the Tabernacle (Exodus 25-40) did not

originate with Moses. Exodus 25:8, 9, 'Then have them make a sanctuary for me, and I will dwell among them. Make this tabernacle and all its furnishings exactly like the pattern I will show you.' When Moses finished all according to God's pattern, God sanctioned the Tabernacle with his Glory.

Exodus 40:34, 35, 'Then the cloud covered the Tent of the Meeting, and the glory of the Lord filled the tabernacle. Moses could not enter the Tent of Meeting because the cloud had settled upon it, and the glory of the Lord filled the tabernacle.'

When we come to the New Testament, the Father's perfect pattern was seen in His Son. He measured up perfectly, and the seal of glory was upon His life and ministry. Many New Testament passages spell this out:

John 1:14, 'The Word became flesh and made his dwelling (tabernacle) among us. We have seen his glory, the glory of the One and Only, who came from the Father, full of grace and truth.'

Colossians 1:19, 'For God was pleased to have all his fullness dwell in him (Jesus).'

Acts 4:12, 'Salvation is found in no one else, for there is no other name under heaven given to men by which we must be saved.'

Revelation 7:10, 'Salvation belongs to our God who sits upon the throne, and to the Lamb.'

Jesus was God's perfect plan. There is no other way, no other gospel.

As we finish this chapter the need to present ourselves to God becomes clearer. Deep down there is an inner temptation to believe that we know how to do God's work and have sufficient spiritual maturity to do it. For all our best intentions there still may be too much sand and not enough rock; too much wood, hay and stubble. And when we present ourselves to God we discover this is true.

'Moses could not enter the Tent of Meeting because the cloud had settled upon it, and the glory of the Lord filled the Tabernacle' Exodus 40:35

CHAPTER 7

Why does God ask us to present ourselves to Him?

Part two

In the previous chapter I gave what I think is one of the most important reasons why God asks us to present ourselves to Him. Namely, that God in these moments reminds us that He anoints with the power of the Holy Spirit, so that His work will be done His way. We can also say that the more our lives change and look like Jesus then the more we are blessed, encouraged, equipped by the Spirit to glorify the Father and bring much fruit to Him.

John 15:8, 'This is to my Father's glory that you bear much fruit, showing yourselves to be my disciples.'

As we look at the life and journey of Moses and Israel, we have an advantage they did not have, that of seeing the various stages of the journey they were about to travel. This is through the courtesy of Leviticus, Numbers and Deuteronomy and the early chapters of Joshua. As we review that journey we will begin to see why it was necessary for God to command that they (and we) present ourselves to him.

Firstly, because they have never been this way before
The difficulty many of us have is that we forget too soon the lessons of yesterday. Even though the exit from Egypt

was not that long ago, a quick replay of the video would soon remind Moses and Israel that they would have never chosen the route of the Red Sea out of Egypt. This scenario would be repeated with Joshua and the entrance into Canaan. Joshua was an exceptional leader; his spirituality, reliability and courage made him the obvious successor to Moses. Despite this, God had to speak directly to him. First of all, He sets out His promises in Joshua 1:

Get ready to cross the Jordan river into the land (verse 2.) I will give you every place where you set your foot (verse 3.) Your territory will extend from the desert to Lebanon, and from the great river, the Euphrates, all the Hittite country, to the Great Sea on the west (verse 5.) No one will be able to stand up against you all the days of your life. As I was with Moses, so I will be with you; I will never leave you nor forsake you (verse .6)

He is to walk by faith. The walk of faith will be met with God's faithfulness, as He demonstrated with Moses. God then begins to emphasize what will be required by Joshua to accomplish this task of entering into the land:

Be strong and courageous (verse 6.) Be strong and very courageous and be careful to obey; do not turn to the right or to the left (verse 7.) Do not let the Book of the Law depart from your mouth; meditate on it day and night, so that you may be careful to do everything written in it (verse 8.) Be strong and courageous; do not be terrified; do not be discouraged (verse 9.)

The answer seems clear. Despite Joshua's past outstanding track record of service, he had not been this way before.

The challenge ahead of God's new day and entry into the land was going to exceed any challenge he had previously encountered. We can ask ourselves the questions about entry into Canaan, and see if we would have ticked all God's boxes.

1. The Timing

Would we have chosen to cross the Jordan when its waters were in spate and at their highest and fiercest? The snow from Mount Hermon had swelled the Jordan to nearly a mile wide. No enemy would attempt to cross the river at this time; it was courting disaster.

2. The Opposition

Would we have thought that Israel was ready to tackle the enemy with its sophisticated weapons of warfare and its seemingly impregnable city, Jericho? True, Joshua had over 600,000 fighting men at his command (Numbers 26:51), but they were inexperienced in warfare. Siege warfare was highly developed, with battering rams, siege towers which they would roll up against the walls, and a device called a turtle. Twenty or thirty men would carry a huge shield which looked like a turtle over them. With this protection, they would attempt to tunnel under the wall to come up inside and take the city from within. The Israelites did not have any understanding of these engines of war.

3. The Method

Would we have chosen the strategy God used? Firstly, suggesting that the priests carry the Ark of the Covenant and walk into the river Jordan, with the belief that as soon as their feet touched the water a miracle would take place? Secondly, by choosing words of a 'faith shout' over and against the most modern weaponry of its day that the enemy had stored up ready to use? Thirdly, knowing that siege warfare could take many years, believe in the quicker option of seeing the walls collapse in a moment and facilitate entry?

The answer most certainly would be no!! As we mentioned earlier, being part of God's new day takes us into spiritual areas that we have never been in before. In the special moments of presenting ourselves to God, we begin to appreciate all that it means to walk by faith and not by sight.

Proverbs 16:25, 'There is a way that seems right to man, but in the end it leads to death.'

Isaiah 55: 8, 9, 'For my thoughts are not your thoughts, neither are your ways my ways,' declares the Lord. 'As the heavens are higher than the earth, so are my ways higher than your ways and my thoughts than your thoughts.'

Isaiah 30:21, 'Whether you turn to the right or to the left, your ears will hear a voice behind you saying, 'This is the way; walk in it.'

No matter how much we nod in agreement or reply that this is common knowledge and basic Christianity, the practical outworking of these scriptures in life and ministry is often quite another thing.

We can be guilty of forging ahead under our own steam and not waiting for the cloud or fire of God's presence. This is the kind of incident we later read about in Numbers.

Numbers 14:40-45
'Early the next morning they went up toward the high hill country. 'We have sinned,' they said. 'We will go up to the place the Lord promised.' But Moses said, 'Why are you

disobeying the Lord's command? This will not succeed! Do not go up, because the Lord is not with you. You will be defeated by your enemies, for the Amalekites and Canaanites will face you there. Because you have turned away from the Lord, he will not be with you and you will fall by the sword.' Nevertheless in their presumption they went up toward the high hill country, though neither Moses nor the ark of the Lord's covenant moved from the camp. Then the Amalekites and Canaanites who lived in that hill country came down and attacked them and beat them down all the way to Hormah.'

The Israelites, having rebelled against the Lord, tried to rectify this and go ahead into the hill country. Despite Moses warning not to do this, as the Lord was not with them, they pressed on. They wanted to try and put things right, and show that to God by their actions. Noble as this may appear, they were simply compounding their disobedience. In their presumption they fought against the Amalekites and Canaanites and were soundly defeated.

> We can be guilty of forging ahead under our own steam and not waiting for the cloud or fire of God's presence

Valedictory service January 1978

At my valedictory service prior to going to Thailand, Len Moules, a remarkable mission leader and statesman known and loved across the mission world, and a man who lived for revival, shared very honestly with me. He spoke on 'If I was a missionary again things would be different'. He recalled the early years of his mission experience in north India. Major Moules the all action man, reaching the unreached, travelling from village to village so that he can record that so many unreached places and people had heard the gospel. The sacrifice made in those tough, rough days in order to fulfil this kind of schedule was huge. I remember him sharing that, as he pursued his vision with all his strength, in order to stem his hunger, he would bite on the leather straps of his bag for several days at a time. Such remarkable commitment and passion, and yet the question remains, 'how would things be different?' Len shared his personal encounter with the Spirit of God and the passage that impacted him so deeply.

Galatians 2:20, 'I have been crucified with Christ, I no longer live, but Christ lives in me. The life I live in the body, I live by faith in the Son of God, who loved me and gave himself for me.'

If Jesus could do nothing in his own strength why am I trying to? If Jesus depended on the Spirit of God to do the will of His Father, surely this is what I should be doing. Whose mission am I involved in, mine or God's?

The change was remarkable as Len encountered the Holy Spirit in a personal and powerful way. He demonstrated from this time on what it was to live in obedience under the clear direction and anointing of the Spirit. These lessons and God given moments only come as we are alone with God, presenting ourselves to Him. For me it was God's special moment. Three weeks later Len went into the presence of God.

Secondly, we can come to the point of being too familiar with our territory and journey

Deuteronomy summarises Israel's journey from Mount Sinai or Horeb to the borders of the Promised Land.

Deuteronomy describes events taking place 40 years after the book of Exodus. During those 40 years an entire generation died. These were the adults who came out of Egypt, crossed the Red Sea, camped at Sinai, and first heard the Ten Commandments. By the time of Deuteronomy they were all dead, with the exception of Moses, Joshua and Caleb.

The new generation needed to be reminded that they must renew their covenant with God, and to get ready to move. It is not God's will to remain at Mount Horeb; there is a land to enter!

Deuteronomy 1:6 ,'The Lord our God said to us at Horeb, 'You have stayed long enough at this mountain.'

Although this story is particular to Moses and Israel, the truth remains that we can get stuck in one place too long. This can be both spiritually and also in our outlook, strategy and ministry. There comes a moment when the Spirit of God begins to dislodge us from our place of comfort, convenience and familiarity. As we present ourselves to God it becomes that moment when, just as the eagle dislodges its chicks from the nest to fly (Deuteronomy 32:11), God does this for us too.

Thirdly, when we present ourselves to God we discover that there is a huge gulf between where we are spiritually and where we need to be to enter the land

Again we have the benefit of understanding and learning from this through the life of Moses and Israel.

The Ten Commandments instruct us how we are to approach God and worship Him. The temptation to breeze in and out of God's presence with little sense of His majesty is very much part of our microwave society.

Leviticus takes us further and focuses on a topic we really do not like too much: holiness. The key word in this book is 'holy' and is mentioned at least 87 times. Holiness means that the God we worship is separated from sin, and is devoted to seeking his own honour. Consequently God then puts the ball back in our court and commands us to be holy too (Leviticus 19:2).

The rich teaching in Leviticus on the sinfulness of man, coupled with God's desire that they demonstrate holiness, love and godliness, is tested as they pursue God's journey into the land. But by the end of Leviticus 27 and up to Numbers chapter 9, they haven't moved anywhere; they are still at Mount Sinai.

Numbers 9:1 gives a time check. It is now one year and one month since Israel left Egypt. They celebrated the Passover with the cloud of God's Presence above the Tabernacle. Then after one year and two months and 20 days the cloud lifted, and they set out from the Desert of Sinai.

Numbers 10:33-36 'So they set out from the mountain of the Lord and travelled for three days. The ark of the covenant of the Lord went before them during those three days to find them a place to rest. The cloud of the Lord was over them by day when they set out from the camp. Whenever the ark set out, Moses said, 'Rise up, O Lord! May your enemies be scattered; may your foes flee before you.' Whenever it came to rest, he said, 'Return, O Lord, to countless thousands of Israel.'

Things looked good at this point. It looked as though they were now ready and sufficient for the task ahead. As I read on about the ensuing struggles in Numbers 11-14 God challenged my own heart, and I became aware yet again of the importance and place of presenting myself to God. God spoke to me:

'It is one thing to experience my Presence, the wonder of those supernatural moments with Me, but how will you react and respond as you hit the road and move out on My journey?'

'How will you react and respond when the going gets tough down in the valley and the opposition appears too much, when even those with you on the journey oppose you?'

'How will you react and respond when the way I want you to go is different from your liking and preference?'

'How will you react and respond when you are out of your comfort zone and travelling in uncharted territory?'

> There is a vast difference between being spiritual in the Tabernacle and being spiritual on God's unfamiliar journey and in enemy territory.

Over the years we have had the privilege of overseeing missionaries and their families in many parts of South-East Asia. Some have come with the highest recommendation and have wonderful testimonies of God's enabling in service. However, travelling from West to East takes them out of their comfort zone both with language and culture. At first the novelty of this new environment brings its own excitement and buzz. Once this has run its course culture shock often kicks in, and it becomes a make or break time.

Many wrestle with God through this testing period. They persevere, discovering a new spiritual hunger and, above the language and cultural adjustment challenge, become aware of their fresh need of the Spirit of God. However, for others this unfamiliar journey, living in a spiritually dark and threatening environment, becomes too much.

Life moving forward on God's journey

An encounter with God goes beyond a precious moment of spiritual blessing. It is to take us on a journey with God. That journey will have many twists and turns, some to our liking and others not. The depth and reality of that encounter will be simply this: 'Not my will but yours be done'.

I find Numbers 11-14 very instructive and challenging, because we begin to monitor life on the journey. How did they respond and react? They complained about hardships (11:1). They were unhappy with their diet (11:4-6). They finished up crying out in self-pity in the entrance of their tents (11:10.)

Those on the mission field have been through this cycle of events over and over again. There are moments when we long for a convenient, comfortable lifestyle; a problem free life with no hardship, persecution and diet change. 'Lord it is not fair, no more Sunday roast, and instead rice and salty fish water'.

On the one hand there are moments when we believe we are ready for whatever God has for us. Then, in the presence of God, the truth makes us see just how vulnerable we are, desiring the pleasures of Egypt on God's supernatural journey.

Even the leadership were affected – Moses himself started to complain to God and drift toward self-pity.

Numbers 11:11-15 'Why have you brought trouble on your servant? What have I done to displease you that you put this burden of all these people on me? Did I conceive all these people? Did I give them birth? Why do you tell me to carry them in my arms, as a nurse carries an infant, to the land you promised on oath to their forefathers? Where can I get meat for all these people? They keep wailing to me, 'Give us meat to eat!' I cannot carry all these people by myself; the burden is too heavy for me. If this is how you are going to treat me, put me to death right now – if I have found favour in your eyes – and do not let me face my own ruin.'

The weight of leadership was taking its toll. The people he was leading had become a 'burden' and a 'rabble'. He then began to doubt God's ability to provide meat for the 600,000 people (Numbers 11:21-22).

Natural ability without anointing
In supervising church planting teams in Asia, the appointment of leadership has obviously been of crucial importance. Church planting, in some of the toughest and most unresponsive parts of the world, has moments of growth and decline, and during these times a change of leadership is often necessary.

Appointing new leaders is an interesting exercise. On most occasions there are those who aspire to leadership and have a thousand and one ideas how to take things forward. Their initial appearance is one of vision, strategy and personal confidence that they are equipped for the task. When not in a leadership position everything seems so easy and straightforward in terms of what needs to be done and how to do it.

As we have supervised these occasions over and over again, a pattern often emerges. When seeking leadership you can see clearly the areas of weakness of the previous leader, and the way things need to change and progress. When in leadership suddenly all those bright ideas seem hollow, and the ability you thought you had seems to have disappeared. Whilst this may seem disastrous, on many occasions it has been the moment for reaching out to God, knowing the need of a new anointing of the Spirit.

Anointing that needs refreshing

Leadership is often a journey of twists and turns, ups and downs, growth and decline. In the majority of cases I see this as more positive than negative. Why? It is not that we have passed our use-by date, but it is a combination of what we have been talking about: we need to realise that familiarity with the task and leadership position has caused us to be becalmed like a yacht with no wind to fill the sails, and we need to realise that this next phase of leadership is beyond anything we have previously experienced.

If what Moses experienced in Numbers 11 wasn't bad enough, things were going to get worse. Miriam and Aaron began to talk against him. Numbers 12:2 'Has the Lord only spoken through you Moses... hasn't he also spoken through us?'

Ten of the twelve leaders exploring the land couldn't get their eyes off the size of the enemy, and in so doing lost sight of God. This went further in chapter 13, and they started to spread rumours of the impossibility of the task considering the size of the enemy (Numbers 13:31-33)

Numbers 14:1-4, 'That night all the people of the community raised their voices and wept aloud. All the Israelites grumbled against Moses and Aaron, and the whole assembly said to them, 'If only we had died in Egypt! Or in this desert! Why is the Lord bringing us to this land only to let us fall by the sword? Our wives and children will be taken as plunder. Wouldn't it be better for us to go back to Egypt? We should choose a leader and go back to Egypt'.

This unrest was about to escalate even more. In Numbers chapter16 Korah rebelled with 250 men against Moses.

There was apparent harmony in the safety of the Tabernacle but all of this took place as they began to travel on God's journey toward the Promised Land.

As I started to process all of this personally, I had a definite sense of God saying, 'Mike, do you now understand why I am asking you to present yourself to Me? Do you not see the clear parallel for today? You have never been this way before. You have become too familiar and comfortable with the journey. You have little idea of the spiritual change that needs to take place. Let me write a new story on the tablet of your heart.'

Proverbs 3:3, 'Let love and faithfulness never leave you; bind them around your neck and write them on the tablet of your heart.'

Jer. 31:33, 'I will put my law in their minds, and write it upon their hearts, I will be their God and they will be my people.'

Ezekiel 36:26, 27, 'I will give you a new heart and put a new spirit in you; I will remove from you your heart of stone and give you a heart of flesh. And I will put my Spirit in you and move you to follow my decrees and be careful to keep my laws.'

2 Cor. 3:3, 'You show that you are a letter from Christ, the result of our ministry, written not with ink but with the Spirit of the living God, not on tablets of stone but on the tablets of human hearts.'

Acts 27:32 seemed to me to have prophetic relevance at

this particular point: 'so the soldiers cut the ropes that held the lifeboat and let it fall away.'

It is a time for cutting away any lifeboat that we may have been tempted to import and tow that would provide an alternative to God's way; and so we pledge before God: 'We will go on Your journey. Lord, will you cleanse the tablet of my heart. Lord, will you write a new story for Your honour and glory.'

From Kadesh to the border was just 11 miles or 17.7 kilometres and yet their time in the desert was extended another 38 years......tragic!!!

God says to us "Let me write a new story, My story, on the tablet of your heart, that you may honour Me."

CHAPTER 8

Presenting ourselves to God is His idea

At this point it may be helpful to consolidate what we have said with regard to presenting ourselves to God. Up to this moment, Moses and Israel have not travelled too far in terms of distance. But they (and now we) have taken the all-important step, beginning to align ourselves to God's heart.

We declare to God that we will prepare a way for God in the desert place, that we will bathe ourselves afresh in the mercy and love of God. We declare that we will, like James McQuilkin, believe that God can bring in His new day again, and we will see each moment as a *kairos* opportunity for God to advance His Kingdom.

We will embrace renewal, hope, revelation and discovery so as to build according to God's divine pattern and experience more of His glory (2 Corinthians 3:18). We will present ourselves to God, recognising our desperate need of His Presence and Spirit for the next phase of life and ministry. We will let every lifeboat, alternative distraction and detour go. Why? Because we know that when we obey and do things His way, He seals our lives with the Spirit of God and His Glory.

At this moment we need to remember that the directive to present ourselves to God comes from God. It was not an optional choice but a command, and it was very personal. 'Moses, listen carefully and obey; present yourself to Me on the top of the mountain' (Exodus 34:2.)

Not wanting to take liberties with the text, I do find myself thinking like this, particularly in an age where commands and directives are not well received. God could have been more 'modern' and said, 'Have a think among yourselves as leaders, see who would like to meet me, and when it is convenient and you are not too busy, then let's arrange a time to get together'.

You and I know that there are moments when commands and directives are essential to heed immediately, whether we like it or not. There are specific moments when you know you cannot get away with anything else than being obedient at once.

I remember as a young management accountant for an international firm receiving a directive from the Chief Executive Officer to be in his office at 9 a.m. Whatever else I had planned to do at 9 o'clock in the morning, however important, had to be put to one side.

In the New Testament Paul uses the Greek word *epitage*. One secular Greek writer says that the acts of the kings of Egypt were held to account by the *epitage* of the law. It is a command that comes from and speaks with the highest authority. It is used in the story of Esther and the royal command coming from King Ahasuerus, and in the command of Nebuchadnezzar to worship his image in the story of Shadrach, Meshach and Abednego. Paul uses *epitage* when he makes a distinction between a human opinion and that which is a direct, revealed command from God. For example, in Romans 16:26 he speaks of the manifestation of Christ to the Gentiles as being in accordance with the *epitage*, the divine command of God. It is a command from the highest authority.

When I reflected on this, I thought to myself, if the CEO had that impact on me, how much more God Himself, the highest possible authority?

No one else – just you and God

Exodus 34:3, 'No one is to come with you or be seen anywhere on the mountain; not even the flocks and herds may graze in front of the mountain.'

The Bible emphasises working together, building together, doing and being church together. The 'one another' verses in Scripture stress that relationship is central to Christianity; firstly a personal relationship with God, and secondly connecting with others, both Christian and non-Christian. The idea of the spiritual hermit and recluse completely detached from others and community life belongs to medieval times. Shortly we will see that the life Jesus lived was full of meaningful relationships, but this was balanced with special times and moments of being alone with His Father.

This was also true for Moses, and I believe for us too. Significant moments of spiritual growth and change mostly involve just God and me. The UK television programme 'Long lost family' seeks to research, find and then re-unite members of a family, some of whom have never met. The hosts offer a last chance for people who are desperate to find long lost relatives. Each relative is guided and supported through the process of tracing the member of their family they have been desperately trying to find. However, in the final moment of meeting and reconciliation they have to face things on their own. It is the same with you and me and God. Our spouses may be so encouraging and supportive, our close friends giving every bit of help, advice and support, our church planting team members may be cheering us on, but the final walk and reconciliation is just God and me, God and you.

Peter an example

Jesus realised that Peter was in danger of shipwrecking his faith when he spoke in Luke 22:31, 32: 'Simon, Simon, Satan has asked to sift you as wheat. But I have prayed for you, Simon, that your faith may not fail. And when you have turned back, strengthen your brothers'.

Peter had made it clear to Jesus that, even if he could not rely on the others, he could rely on him. He would never fall away (Mark 14:29). However, in the extreme pressure of the moment, and at the risk of being identified as a disciple of Jesus, Peter denied the Lord three times.

In John 21 after Jesus' resurrection he meets the disciples by the Sea of Galilee. Having recognised him, they come ashore to find that Jesus had prepared a fish barbecue on the beach for them all; this would have brought him much pleasure. But John makes sure that it does not finish there, but with Peter meeting Jesus face to face.

These moments on our own with the Lord can be painful times, but in and through them he prepares us for His new day. Jesus restored Peter and his call to leadership and ministry and his place as a future apostle to the Jews and leader of the Jerusalem church.

Jesus Himself modelled a balanced lifestyle but knew his priority

Jesus enjoyed his relationship with his disciples, especially Peter, James and John. They were with him every day.

The home of Lazarus, Mary and Martha was very special to him, to enjoy their hospitality and friendship. But he knew when to withdraw from the crowds to be alone with His Father. He made statements like 'My food is to do the will of him who sent me and to finish his work' (John 4:34). 'I tell you the truth, the Son can do nothing by himself; he can do only what he sees his Father doing, because whatever the Father does the Son also does' (John 5:19).

The significant moments that kept Jesus walking in obedience to the Father and in tune with the Holy Spirit came out of moments of being alone with His Father. Mark 1:35, 'Very early in the morning, while it was still dark, Jesus got up, left the house and went off to a solitary place, where he prayed.'

We say that there is safety in numbers, and in certain circumstances this may be true. But there are special moments when you can't call on the services or even advice of your closest colleagues, wife or husband; it has to be God and you, God and me! God's timing is now to meet him in a personal, intimate way.

God loves to do new things

In presenting ourselves to God, it is not just about sorting out our lives, examination and evaluation. This will be part of it, because as we mentioned earlier from Malachi, 'he will be like a refiner's fire' (Malachi 3:2).

When Paul talks about how wide and long and high and deep is the love of God in Christ (Ephesians 3:18) it is so that we are caught up in the extravagant love of God, who longs for us to be filled with the measure of all the fullness of God.

Throughout Scripture God declares that He is a God

who loves to do new things. In fact, it began with Him creating heaven and earth and man in his image, and it will finish with Him recreating a new heaven and earth and man into the perfect image of His Son Jesus.

Restoration and recreation are a central aspect of the heart of God and the Christian hope. And in between the beginning and the end, God's promises ring out, one of the most well-known being Isaiah 43:18, 19, 'Forget the former things; do not dwell on the past. See, I am doing a new thing! Now it springs up; do you not perceive it? I am making a way in the desert and streams in the wasteland.'

God's new day appeared supremely in the coming of Jesus. His coming means that nothing will ever be the same again, bringing life and salvation, a sure hope and a future which even death cannot defeat. In the New Testament there are two words for 'new'.

New in quality (*kainos*) in contrast with the old

- new birth, new life, new creation through the Gospel (2 Corinthians 5:17)
- a new covenant (Luke 22:20)
- a new commandment (John 13:34)
- a new song (Revelation 5:9)
- a new name (Revelation 2:17)
- new wine and a new wineskin (Luke 5:38)

New in respect to time (*neos*), that which is recent

- the new man in Colossians 3:10 stresses the fact of the believer's new experience, recently begun but still carrying on

- the new wine of Matthew 9:17; Mark 2:22; Luke 5:37–39 is new, produced recently and freshly experienced

The God who loves to do new things will combine both of these. The 'new man' in Ephesians 2:15 (*kainos*) receives new quality of life. The 'new man' in Colossians 3:10 (*neos*) receives new experiences as Paul teaches in 2 Corinthians 3:18. All the promises of God are in the present continuous tense until we become like Jesus; a constant, glorious change taking place day by day.

When we mention the word 'new' let's be clear; we are not saying that what has happened is second best – far from it. But my take on it is this: that when we are brought by the grace and mercy of God into His new day, yesterday, for all its blessing and wonder, will look 'old' in the light of the present work and manifestation of the Spirit.

We can understand this when we compare the Old with the New Testament. The revelation of the Holy Spirit in the Old Testament is truly spectacular – just look at God's revelation to Isaiah in chapters 40–60! But when we compare that to the revelation of the Holy Spirit in the New Testament it becomes like Moses' glory, fading, in comparison with the glory and radiance of Jesus the Son of God. Paul teaches about this in 2 Corinthians 3 and 4.

A new day in Sukhothai

I referred earlier to my time in Sukhothai, the ancient capital of Thailand. The man who came to Christ and later became an elder in the church was called Chalerm. When he came to faith his wife, a keen Buddhist, was very angry with me. In fact, despite the many positive changes she saw in him, she still wished he had not believed in Jesus. However, after a few weeks she too came to faith, and joined Chalerm in the new life Jesus gives.

This was truly wonderful, but the effect on the children made a deep impact on me. Prior to believing, Chalerm would often come home drunk, and the house was far from being a happy place, the children having to hide from their father. However, the work of the Spirit in his life had already begun to form a new family. I can still remember the day when their youngest son, called number one, jumped into my arms and said, 'Thank you for a new mummy and daddy; I now no longer need to hide when my father returns home. I can't wait for all of us to be at home together'.

These moments are still very precious, and they remind me today of my God who still loves to do new things. I am so glad that I did present myself on that mountain top outside Chiangmai, so that God could do His new thing in me and through me. And as I reflect back to that time I become aware of my need to obey His command and to present myself to Him again.

You and I know that there are moments when commands and directives are essential to heed immediately whether we like it or not. That time for Moses and us is 'now.'

CHAPTER 9

How did this impact Moses, Joshua and Israel?

The subject of presenting ourselves to God is not an isolated one in Scripture, nor is it to be a one-off occasion. Throughout the pages of Scripture and down through the centuries men and women have been instructed, challenged and encouraged to present themselves to God at crucial times in their lives.

The aim at this point is not to give a detailed study of what this actually means. My desire is to look at the impact this moment can have on our lives.

The temptation to accept second best is very much part of spiritual warfare. This is especially so when going through a tough time, be it physically or spiritually. We can fall into thinking that perhaps this is my lot and I should just be grateful for what I have received and experienced, and leave it at that. Alternatively, we might convince ourselves that we are genuinely satisfied with our walk with God and content with what we are doing for Him.

I have come to realise that my missionary and ministry journey can either be defined as 'wandering in the desert' or 'crossing over into the land'. Please understand me; I am not being ungrateful nor am I trying to be super-spiritual. I am truly grateful to the Lord for all the years where His grace and mercy have been so evident. I am truly grateful for every moment when the Spirit of God has opened my understanding to His Word; when the piece of truth presented to me has become a 'wow' moment. I am truly grateful for those occasions when the Spirit of God has been so real and close that He has melted my heart, tears have flowed and I have been on my face before God.

But I want to be real and admit that, despite such moments, the natural me still drifts towards being content with wandering in the desert. That is, experiencing occasional moments of God's supernatural provision, presence and help. If I am honest, that is all I am really expecting, even though I know that this is God's second best.

In Chapter One we saw how the desert can cause our spiritual lives to become so discouraged that we are tempted to give up; now the challenge is related to accepting second best. Remember that for Moses and Israel the desert had its own very special moments – God regularly provided for His people and his presence was at times very powerful. Just think how amazing it would have been to see the glory of the Lord settle on the tabernacle, or the pillar of fire that led them by night.

For many of us, if we are honest, these God moments might convince us that the desert is not a bad place after all – who needs to bother with entering into the land? Being content with second best will surely leave the heart of God saddened and disappointed that we never had the courage and faith to trust in Him and walk in obedience out of our comfort zones and across into the land.

Before we look in detail at how Moses presented himself to God, here are some questions we should ask ourselves:

1. Am I content with my present life and ministry? Reflection: How much is my current ministry and spiritual life focussed on me rather than God?
2. Will my life be defined by desert wandering or by crossing the river into the land? Reflection: What is holding me back, and what changes need to take place to enable me to leave the valleys and take the hill country, like Caleb?
3. What would a new day of life and ministry in the Spirit be like to me, especially if I am a leader? Reflection: What do I really believe God longs to do in me and through me?

The heart of Moses' spiritual encounter

It seems to me a miracle that Moses overcame the acute disappointment of Numbers 20:1-13 when he struck the rock in disobedience with a devastating result. It is truly amazing that he remained so loyal to his people, for they were guilty of criticizing him, rebelling against him, and lying to him. And despite knowing that he would not enter Canaan, he did everything possible to enable Israel to do so. Moses remained faithful to the Lord (Heb. 3:1-6), and this is why he continued to the end to be faithful to Israel.

When we present ourselves to God what follows is not primarily about you or me but God.

As Moses presented himself before God there are three things that impacted Moses himself, Israel, Joshua and me, especially when I look at the quality of leadership required to lead on into the land.

1. <u>His ministry was solely for God and directed by God</u>
When we respond to God's command and present ourselves in obedience to Him, then, something emerges that will

be a thousand miles higher than anything else. This life and ministry is about God and Him alone. It is about being directed, led and anointed by God, and about obedience.

I would love to be able to ask Moses some questions:

- When you presented yourself to God what kind of blessing were you hoping for?
- Was there an internal battle going on, flesh versus Spirit?
- If you are honest, was your primary desire for some special anointing so that your leadership would be elevated to a new level and people would see and recognise your spirituality?
- Was there an element of 'what's in it for me?' Eternal gain is amazing, but didn't you think about the short term, and enjoying the here and now benefits and acclaim?
- Am I the only one prone to this, or were you too?

How can Moses be such an amazing leadership example? After all, in Numbers 20:1-13 we read of an incident in which Moses disobeyed God's instructions, and struck the rock instead of speaking to it. The result was that he was only allowed to look into the land and not enter it personally.

Deuteronomy 32:48-52
'On that same day the Lord told Moses, 'Go up into the Abarim Range to Mount Nebo in Moab, across from Jericho, and view Canaan, the land I am giving the Israelites as their own possession. There on the mountain that you have climbed you will die and be gathered to your people, just as your brother Aaron died on Mount Hor and was gathered to his people. This is because both of you broke faith with me in the presence of the Israelites at the waters

of Meribah Kadesh in the Desert of Zin and because you did not uphold my holiness among the Israelites. Therefore you will see the land only from a distance; you will not enter the land I am giving to the people of Israel.'

God's directions are clearly stated in Numbers 20:8. Moses is to take the staff, assemble the people, and speak to the rock. Instead, he assembles the people, speaks to the people and strikes the rock with his staff. The act of striking, and especially with two strokes, not only shows his irritation with the people (reflected in Numbers 20:10.... 'must we fetch you water out of this rock?'), but it caused the people to transfer their gaze to him and his leadership, rather than have their eyes fixed on God. It prevented the full power and holiness of God from being clearly evident to the people.

Why then is his leadership an example?

Am I sanctioning disobedience? Of course not! As we point the finger at Moses we must remember that three fingers point back at ourselves. I am reminded of the words of Jesus to the teachers of the law and to the Pharisees in John chapter eight. They wanted to stone the woman caught in adultery, and Jesus said, 'If any of you is without sin let him be the first to throw a stone at her'.

Adopting a Pharisaic stance is all too easy, presenting a 'holier than thou' attitude, only for us to realise the need to put stones down and meekly walk away, with moments of personal disobedience being all too apparent. Moses' acts of disobedience are a timely reminder to all of us that entering into the land, God's new day, demands total obedience, giving Him all the glory, and being very careful in even the smallest and seemingly insignificant aspects of life. In Song of Solomon 2:15 they are referred to as 'little foxes that destroy the vineyard'. When the Spirit of God begins to move us on His journey, there is a conviction at a level much deeper than we have ever known before. Aspects of life which previously had not bothered us too much, for example, exaggeration, inflating our own importance and spirituality, impatience, irritability and overconfidence in our own ability, can become the little foxes that keep our lives from being fruitful in God's vineyard.

> This act of disobedience with its costly outcome did not dampen or lessen Moses' enthusiasm and dedication to fulfil God's vision. He was as committed after the failure of Numbers 20:1-13 as he was before.

Personal challenges

At a leadership level, whilst I can try and put a spiritual mask on my face, I believe that my response would have been significantly more about me than God. I find it incredibly difficult to think about God first and foremost; such is the frailty of our humanity. We sing the song 'It's all about you Jesus', but once back in the marketplace there is a huge struggle to embrace this in daily life and ministry.

As I read from Exodus 34 to the end of Moses' days I am absolutely in awe of his leadership. Whilst we do not know exactly what took place in that mountain encounter, one thing seems apparent: everything about Moses' life and ministry was consumed with God and His vision, will and purpose. In other words it was all about entering into the land God had promised.

As I contemplate wandering in the desert versus entering into the land, I am aware of those who were so open to the

Spirit of God that their personal interest, at whatever level, was of little concern to them.

(i) David Brainerd (1718-1747)

As a young man preparing to go to the mission field, the life of David Brainerd made a huge impression upon me. Dying so young and yet accomplishing so much. If ever a man displayed the desire to leave the desert and enter the land it was him. But what impressed me was not only his evangelistic success and revival amongst the American Indians but his heart for God. He writes on one occasion:

> *'Had the most ardent longings after God that ever I felt in my life: at noon, in my secret retirement, I could do nothing but tell my dear Lord, in a sweet calm, that he knew I longed for nothing but himself, nothing but holiness; that he had given me these desires, and he only could give me the thing desired. I never seemed to be so unhinged from myself, and to be so wholly devoted to God. My heart was swallowed up in God most of the day. In the evening I had such a view of the soul being as it were enlarged, to contain more holiness, that it seemed ready to separate from my body'.*

(ii) Granny Brand (1879-1974)

Evelyn Constance Harris was born in May 1879, and grew up in the fashionable St. John's Wood area of London. Her father saw that she had the best of education suitable to young ladies of that time.

Later she heard Jesse Mann Brand speak of the neglected hill people of south India, steeped in Hinduism, sin, and poverty. Her heart was drawn out to these people, whose home was on the Kolli Moloi 'mountains of death,' so named because of the many diseases and particularly deadly malaria that ravaged them. She volunteered for missionary service to these needy people.

After a short course on tropical diseases, she proceeded to India in 1912. Here again she met Jesse Brand, and they were married in August 1913.

Jesse was a man with many talents: doctor, dentist, preacher, teacher, counsellor, agronomist, builder; all things to all men. His medical skills broke down barriers. Their first convert was a lad whose salvation brought great joy to their hearts, but he died very soon of pneumonia. It was six long years until the next fruit came from their labours. The work among the hill people progressed, and a church with outstations was established.

Jesse was rarely ill, but in July 1929 he came down with a severe bout of malaria that soon turned into black water fever. He died, and his body was buried on the 'mountains of death.' Evelyn was devastated and alone.

During the war years, the mission board would not let her go back to the mountains with the unrest and the division between India and Pakistan.

Finally, in 1947, what she called a 'new birth' occurred. India became an independent nation. Evelyn went to a new range of mountains. She built a small mud hut for a home, and tirelessly ministered to these neglected people.

In 1953 Granny fell in her home and fractured her hip. At 74 years of age, she was a feisty old lady, very dedicated to the task to which God had called her. Many tried to persuade her to retire from the rigours of mountain life and come live with them in a comfortable home. She would have none of it.

In 1963, at the age of 84, she moved to a third range of mountains, and in 1965, after working alone in the mountains for almost 35 years, a missionary nurse was assigned to work with her as her companion until the time of her death.

She wrote to her son Paul shortly before her 95th birthday. She was sure a lot of kindly people would write and praise her and say how wonderful she was to be working still. She said, 'I am not wonderful. I am just a poor, old, frail, and weak woman. God has taken hold of me and gives me the strength I need each day. He uses me just because I know that I have no strength of my own. Please tell the people to praise God, not me.'

Soon afterwards she died, and her frail, wasted body was carried back and buried beside her beloved Jesse.

David Brainerd and Granny Brand are just two examples of many who have been transformed by the Spirit of God to follow Jesus and give their lives out of sacrificial love.

- totally unhinged from themselves
- their hearts swallowed up by God

(iii) <u>Adoniram Judson, Jr.</u> (August 9, 1788 – April 12, 1850) Judson served in Burma for almost 40 years. Before he reached Burma, he was told that the Buddhist people would not respond to Christianity. Judson, who already knew Latin, Greek, and Hebrew, immediately began studying the Burmese grammar, but took over three years learning to speak it. He found a tutor and spent twelve hours per day studying the language. He and his wife firmly dedicated themselves to understanding it.

First attempts by the Judsons to interest the people

of Rangoon with the gospel of Jesus met with almost total indifference. Buddhist traditions and the Burmese worldview at that time led many to disregard the pleadings of Adoniram and his wife to believe in one living and all-powerful God. To add to their discouragement, their second child, Roger William Judson, died at almost eight months of age.

We would have understood if, at this point, Judson had washed his hands of mission in Burma. The people's hearts were just too hard! Like Moses with Israel, he could have justifiably dismissed the Burmese and given up on them.

However, that was not the case. No matter how rebellious the people were in those difficult early days, he had encountered God, and nothing would deter him from following His calling.

When Judson began his mission in Burma, he set a goal of translating the Bible and founding a church of 100 members before his death. When he died, he left the Bible, 100 churches, and over 8,000 believers!

(iv) Jesus

Of course head and shoulders above everyone else is Jesus Himself. He was filled with the fullness of the Spirit of God, an encounter Luke tells us that opened up heaven. Let's just remind ourselves of a few sayings of Jesus from John's Gospel that define so clearly His life and ministry, anointed by the Holy Spirit.

John 4:34, 'My food,' said Jesus, 'is to do the will of him who sent me and to finish his work.'

John 5:30, 'By myself I can do nothing; I judge only as I hear, and my judgment is just, for I seek not to please myself but him who sent me.'

John 6:38, 'For I have come down from heaven not to

do my will but to do the will of him who sent me.'

John 14:31, 'but the world must learn that I love the Father and that I do exactly what my Father has commanded me.'

It is this level of selfless obedience to the will of the Father that purchased our redemption. Delivering the demonic, healing the sick and acts of compassion were important, but obedience in Jesus' life and ministry was supreme above all else.

Will your obedience to the will of the Father be supreme? Or will the anointing of the Spirit for powerful and effective ministry tip the balance and become number one?

The world today is putting pressure and demands upon the church to live in a way that they feel comfortable with. Will I succumb to this or will I remain faithful to the will, purpose and mission of God?

Moses is known as a teacher, intercessor, prophet, deliverer, judge, shepherd, writer and mediator – quite an amazing list of gifting. But what is it that stands out a thousand miles higher than anything else? Moses' level of obedience was astounding, whether in big matters or seemingly small and trivial ones. We must not forget that Moses was a very intelligent man who had a great education. Most likely he would have had a million ideas, his personal preferences, and his strategic plans. Yet he obeyed God, and the examples are endless; from arranging the camp and maintaining the level of purity within it, to responsibility for the tabernacle and the need for the Ark to go before them.

Familiar words of challenge ring out through Moses in Deuteronomy 11 and 28: 'be careful... do not forget... watch out'. All these challenges are summarised in one verse:

Deut. 4:9 'Only be careful and watch yourselves closely so that you do not forget the things your eyes have seen or let them slip from your heart as long as you live.'

Perhaps at this point we should take time to reflect again that God has a pattern in all He does. I referred to this earlier, and this truth is clearly displayed through the Old and the New Testaments. The glory of God only descends according to the divine pattern or way of doing things. As I mentioned earlier, neither a heap of stones nor a pile of materials on a piece of land is a house. In the same way, a church is not a church just because 300 people attend every week. All must be assembled and built according to the plan of the Architect.

This is the challenge coming from Moses' life. Second best may satisfy us but will not satisfy God. Godly leadership is only content with doing things God's way. The willingness to sacrifice will display the depth of our love for God.

When we come to the New Testament the Father's perfect pattern was seen in His Son. He measured up perfectly and the seal of glory was upon His life and ministry.

As we reflect on the lives of David Brainerd, Granny Brand and supremely Jesus, a question remains in the forefront of my mind: 'How much of my spiritual life is about me rather than God?'

2. <u>Moses lived for God's people to enter the land, even though he never would!</u>
This had to come out of his encounter with God on the mountain. This kind of sacrificial, selfless service only comes from a supernatural encounter with God. It is not manufactured out of the goodness of a person's own heart.

It seems to me that this is the heart of a leader, and a Christ-like response from encountering God in a personal manner. Moses could have justifiably dismissed Israel, and given up on them entering into the land. After all, look at their behaviour!

As for Israel, their period of wandering in the wilderness falls into three parts: the three-month journey from the Red Sea to Sinai, the two-year encampment at Sinai, and wandering 38 years before entering the Promised Land.

Disobedience and rebellion characterise each of these periods. They complained and quarrelled about food and water. They wanted to return to Egypt. Later, even Miriam and Aaron opposed Moses. The people rebelled against the leadership because of the size of the enemy. They acted presumptuously, believing God was with them, and were defeated in battle. 250 well-known community leaders from the house of Korah rebelled, opposing Aaron and Moses.

Why would you continue to lead such a people? Why would you continue to pour the remaining years of your life out on this kind of people? I can only find one explanation: Jesus expressed it beautifully: 'For even the Son of Man did not come to be served, but to serve, and to give his life as a ransom for many' (Mark 10:45).

For Paul it was enough to imitate his master. He wrote, 'I have been crucified with Christ and I no longer live, but Christ lives in me. The life I live in this body, I live by faith in the Son of God, who loved me and gave himself for me' (Galatians 2:20).

How can you explain this? There is no other way other than by a deep, life-changing moment or moments of supernatural encounter with God.

It has often been said that in leadership character comes before charisma. Moses had charisma (very necessary), but character, allowing God to have his way at whatever personal cost, was a thousand miles higher.

3. Moses lived to give the people the godly leadership they needed to enter the land

How Moses inwardly felt about being excluded from entering the land we do not know, but Deuteronomy 28–34 is an amazing portion of Scripture and gives us a clear idea of his focus as a leader. His submission to the will of God and his obedience at whatever personal cost was the foundation of his life. Out of this the blessings flowed. He saw God open the storehouse of heaven, providing food, water and daily needs. He saw God restoring His Presence in the midst of the people. He experienced victory over much more powerful enemies. The passion of his heart was to communicate the need to remember to be careful; to love, obey, follow and to choose life over death. His focus was: live, increase and occupy the land. No wonder at the close of his life he puts all of this into a song.

Deuteronomy 31 takes us into the third area of importance.

New leadership for the new land

Moses repeats what the Lord spoke to him: 'You shall not cross the Jordan' (verse 2). It sets into motion a new day of leadership. But before we look at that briefly we need to remind ourselves that Joshua and the people would not be the first to cross over the Jordan. 'The Lord your God will cross over ahead of you'.

It makes us ask two questions related to moving forward, expanding, growing, and occupying the land.

Question 1: **Where has God gone ahead of us and prepared the way?**

How the Spirit speaks this to us can come in a multitude of ways. For Paul it was through a vision. He wanted to go into Asia (Acts 16:6), and when he came to the border of Mysia he tried to enter Bithynia. But in the night he had a vision of a man from Macedonia saying, 'Come over and help us'.

Question 2: **Who has God ordained to lead into this new day?**

God sets aside people for different stages of his mission. Peter was to see the Jerusalem church born, and then expand into Judea and Samaria. The next stage was for Paul and Barnabas: 'Set apart for me Barnabas and Saul for the work to which I have called them' (Acts 13:2).

In Numbers 12:3 Moses is described as a meek and humble man, more so than any other person on the face of the earth. Meekness is an attitude of humble, submissive and expectant trust in God, and a loving, patient and gentle attitude toward others.

Moses, in taking delight and personal pride in preparing Joshua to succeed him, displays this attitude so clearly. Was there an internal struggle? We do not know. Was there a sense of regret? No doubt from a human perspective there was.

At this point so many 'what ifs' come to mind. What if he had insisted in remaining in leadership? What if he had refused to accept that his leadership had run its course? What if he had allowed pride to surge into pole position? After all, his eyes were not weak nor his strength gone (Deuteronomy 34:7).

In Chapter One I mentioned about my leadership struggle with the Church in Bangkok. What if I had tried to portray an 'I should always be the leader and be in control' attitude? What if I had not seen that my role in leading a church in Thailand needed to be transferred to Thai leaders? What if, in an attempt to prove myself able, I had clung on to leadership? The answer came back so clearly: 'The church would never have grown the way it did?' Again, the mercy and grace of God comes to the fore, and Moses is such an inspirational example.

Woven into these two questions 'Where has God gone ahead of us and prepared the way?' and 'Who has God ordained to lead into this new day?' is the command of God. Moses received this and he also passed it on to Joshua. It is imperative to any successful venture.

> 'Be strong and courageous. Do not be afraid or terrified because of them (opposition) for the Lord your God goes with you; he will never leave you nor forsake you' (Deut. 31:6)

Moses shows his maturity and godliness in the way he responded to not being allowed to enter the land with the people. His eyes were fixed on God and His way forward for the people. It concludes this chapter where the emphasis has been on sacrificial leadership, so much reflecting the perfect example of Jesus.

Moses prays: 'May the Lord God of the spirits of all mankind appoint a man over this community to go out and come in before them, one who will lead them out and bring them in, so that the Lord's people will not be like sheep without a shepherd'. (Numbers 27:15-17)

God answers, 'Take Joshua son of Nun, a man in whom is the spirit, and lay hands on him' (Numbers 27:18).

Why Joshua? He had proved himself as a man with a *servant heart* in the tribe of Ephraim. He had proved himself as a man who *loved the presence of God* and worship (Exodus 33:11). He had proved himself as *a man of faith and courage* (Numbers 14:6-9). He was a man with a <u>sensitive</u> <u>heart</u>, tearing his clothes in an act of repentance at any sign of rebellion toward God (Numbers 14:6). He was a man who *understood that his own morality needed to be of the highest level*. After all, he was leading the people of God. Their level of morality and holiness before God would affect their success in battle and their entry into the land. He was commissioned not only by Moses but by God Himself (Deut. 31:14.)

The legacy of godly leadership is that both Moses and Joshua finished well! They didn't give in to personal failure, criticism and discouragement. They didn't allow the size and power of the enemy to make them doubt that their God was far above all. They didn't give up even when the people they were leading disobeyed God. They continued to live the life and speak the truth with courage, faith and anointing, and above all they walked humbly before God. And so Israel entered the land.

Moses finished reciting the song of Deuteronomy 32 and blessing each tribe.

Joshua finished with a clear clarion call to the nation to yield their hearts to God in Joshua 24.

<u>The deep impact of the Spirit in Moses' encounter:</u>

1. His ministry was solely for God and directed by God.
2. He lived for God's people to enter the land even though he never would!
3. He lived to give the people the godly leadership they needed to enter the land

---

CONCLUSION...

Consecrate yourselves for tomorrow

I have been in awe of Moses and his leadership. It began with a man who had been on the run having murdered an Egyptian. Who would have thought that God would have been interested in a man like this? His supernatural encounter with God at the burning bush resurrected Moses from the grave of defeat and hopelessness to an exhilarating walk with God that was to take Israel through the desert and into the land of promise – God's new day.

In my first book *Out of the Desert* and now *Into the Land* my desire has not been to stimulate just the mind, but that the Spirit of God will stir our hearts, then renew our minds, enabling us to look beyond the desert into the land and God's new day. It is this new day that has caught my heart.

Remember, this is a day of heaven being opened and darkness being pushed back. It is a day of seeing the glory of God, and hearing the voice of God speak clearly and powerfully. It is a day when hardened, cynical, despising hearts are wonderfully changed, as young and old, rich and poor, become aware that today God's mercy and grace can still be received, and His day of salvation has not passed them by.

This is a day when we in the church not only believe in Jesus as Saviour but also as Lord, and the one who has the right to direct and guide every aspect of our lives. It is a day when the church awakens out of its cosy, fireside comfort, to reach out into a cold world that needs to hear the Gospel, the Good News, and see the transforming change that comes to lives who accept Him on His terms. It is a day when we see ourselves not just as believers but as disciples, walking in the footsteps of Jesus' life and ministry, whatever the cost. And it is a day when people are talking of their personal need of Jesus, and not denouncing and denying Him.

My heart's sincere cry is that my life and ministry will not be defined as wandering in the desert but entering into the land. What about you?

The question is, 'What do we do, then?'

Let's recap:

- Learn from the desert but do not live there; move on!
- Allow the Word and the Spirit to remove every obstacle, make the rough ground smooth, level the mountains and raise up the valleys.
- Remember that God promises to turn the darkness into light.
- Humble yourself in the tough place so that in due time, God's time, He may lift you up.
- Lift up your voice and sing. Sing!
- He will take hold of you by the hand and help you; do not fear.
- Hear God speaking: 'Just come with clean and empty tablets so that I can write a new story on your heart'.
- Be ready ... be prepared ... present yourself to God.
- Listen to James McQuilkin: 'If God has visited His people before, why not again?'

- Live for God; be obedient to His vision and mission! It is not about you or me.
- Serve God's people!
- Prepare God's leaders for His tomorrow!
- Finish well!

Moses did just that. He prepared the way for God to anoint Joshua for entry into the land. If the Spirit is similarly speaking to you, then prepare the way for others just as Moses did for Joshua.

Joshua picked up God's baton for the next stage of the race and journey into the land. Despite his experience and impeccable servant record, he had never been this way before; and neither have you or I. He rallied Israel in the face of overwhelming opposition, to consecrate themselves to God. We finish with his words:

> 'Consecrate yourselves, for tomorrow the Lord will do amazing things among you.' Joshua 3:5

If you are like Joshua, about to pick up that baton, then put yourself in the position where God's mercy, grace, power and might can flow through you. Walk in obedience and humility into the land of His promise, remembering that now is the time to present yourself to God.